The Horse Owner's ESSENTIAL Survival Guide

Susan McBane

contents

SUSAN McBANE began riding at the age of four and has owned and cared for horses, from ponies to racehorses, all her life. A clear communicator, Susan has used her equestrian experience to write more than 40 books. She has acted as a consultant to private and commercial clients, legal practices, book publishers and the BBC Natural History Unit. Her practical approach to life and her enthusiasm make this an encouraging book for those of us who feel the rising tide of disorganization!

A DAVID & CHARLES BOOK
Copyright © David & Charles Limited 2004, 2007

David & Charles is an F+W Publications Inc. company
4700 East Galbraith Road
Cincinnati, OH 45236

First published in 2004
Reprinted 2004, 2005
First paperback edition 2007

Copyright © Susan McBane 2004, 2007

Susan McBane has asserted her right to be identified as author of this work in accordance with the Copyright, Designs and Patents Act, 1988. All rights reserved. No part of this publication may be reproduced, stored in a retrieval system, or transmitted, in any form or by any means, electronic or mechanical, by photocopying, recording or otherwise, without prior permission in writing from the publisher.

Horse care and riding are not without risk, and while the author and publishers have made every attempt to offer accurate and reliable information to the best of their knowledge and belief, it is presented without any guarantee. The author and publishers therefore disclaim any liability incurred in connection with using the information contained in this book.

A catalogue record for this book is available from the British Library.

ISBN-13: 978-0-7153-1649-8 hardback
ISBN-10: 0-7153-1649-4 hardback

ISBN-13: 978-0-7153-2787-6 paperback
ISBN-10: 0-7153-2787-9 paperback

Printed in China by Hong Kong Graphics Ltd. for David & Charles
Brunel House   Newton Abbot   Devon

Visit our website at www.davidandcharles.co.uk

David & Charles books are available from all good bookshops; alternatively you can contact our Orderline on 0870 9908222 or write to us at FREEPOST EX2 110, D&C Direct, Newton Abbot, TQ12 4ZZ (no stamp required UK only); US customers call 800-289-0963 and Canadian customers call 800-840-5220.

before you start

Most new horse owners get a terrific shock when they realise just how much time a horse of their own takes up, compared to 'playing' with riding centre or friends' horses. Ignorance was bliss; now you've just got to get on with it.

This book has been written for busy horse owners who keep their horses on do-it-yourself (DIY) livery or (the lucky few) at home outside their own back doors. Most 'ordinary' owners have to work, not only to keep themselves, but also their horse, or horses, too. As good livery stables are still generally very thin on the ground, and full and part livery is expensive, many people choose DIY livery so they know that at least the basic tasks required to care for their horse have been done. But because of work commitments, they often feel that the jobs are not all being done in the way that they should be.

Time and money are the two things working owners are usually short of – and the two things horses need a lot of. It is easy to become bogged down trying to keep up with other people's standards and attitudes (particularly those put into print by 'establishment' equestrian organizations). Many people are more conformist than they need to be and too worried about doing things 'correctly'. Consequently, they are rushed off their feet most of the time as they try to fit in their job, their horse, their domestic responsibilities, their family and some kind of social life, let alone other hobbies. You are not the only horse owner to feel you need 48 hours in every day, plus two pairs of hands and legs, never mind two heads. There are, though, many ways to cut down on the hands-on work and expense involved in caring for a horse. It is possible to juggle a job, family, social life and horses without any of them suffering, you just have to adjust your attitude and rethink your approach.

The section on prioritizing jobs (pp.66–69) is the most important in helping you manage to balance your horse time with your other commitments, and is the real key to keeping a horse truly well on limited time. There are also flow charts on disorders to help owners make an accurate decision about whether or not an expensive veterinary visit is needed or whether the matter can safely wait (pp.144–147). The cash-saving tips help you make the very best of your budgets and buying power, too.

If you're a bit horrified on first reading the book, lie down for a while or have a stiff drink, then go through the 'worst' bits again. I can assure you that the methods described have stood the test of time. They've worked for many people and they'll work for you – and your horse.

Susan McBane

1

Consider Management

In the horse world there is a well-worn saying that is very true:

Each horse is an individual and must be treated as such.

It is also true that there are certain set methods and procedures to follow when looking after horses. These are widely accepted and used and are detailed in most good books on horse care. However, a routine that suits one animal perfectly may be anathema to another and it is the owner's or attendant's ability – *and willingness* – to adapt existing systems of management to suit his or her particular horse, facilities and circumstances that determine how successful he or she will be as a horsemaster. Between the individuality of a particular horse and the uniformity of a set system of management lies the secret of keeping a horse happy, healthy and well.

In the case of someone who can spend only limited time looking after a horse because of work and other commitments, it is particularly important that the horse and the system adopted are compatible because you will not be there most of the time to cater for the horse's needs. It is no use, for instance, trying to make an active, athletic type of horse who is always full of energy (nervous or feed-induced) exist under a system where he spends 23 out of his 24 hours stabled. It would also be ineffective and maybe even cruel to keep out at grass the type of animal who curls up at the first sign of wind or rain.

Let us, therefore, look at the various systems of horse management, the advantages and disadvantages of each and how we can relate them to horses' differing constitutions and temperaments.

management systems

stabled

HAVING A HORSE entirely or almost entirely stabled is obviously the most tying, time-consuming and expensive way of keeping him. It is not, though, necessarily much more expensive than yarding or corralling a horse or keeping him at grass, as these facilities may have to be rented. In addition, yarded horses have to be fed in the same way as stabled horses all year round and in winter grass-kept horses will probably need more food than stabled ones to keep out the cold.

A stabled horse has to have everything done for him by his human attendants. In particular, it may be very difficult for an owner with limited time to give him enough exercise to keep him even healthy, never mind content. Every day, a stabled horse, even an unfit one, needs a few hours' exercise, ideally in two sessions, to maintain his health. This does not only mean being given ridden or driven exercise, but also general moving about, either at liberty or through being walked out in hand, lunged, long-reined or worked loose (which doesn't mean chased about at high speeds). Older horses who become very fond of their stables still need to be exercised regularly and gently for frequent, shortish stints to keep them mobile, functional and occupied. For the busy owner of a stabled horse, a mechanical horsewalker, used in moderation, can be a good time-saver.

In addition to the pressure of making sure he has enough exercise, you need to make sure your horse is groomed regularly to prevent excessive build-up of dandruff and grease in his coat as he is not exposed to rain nor can he roll as easily as when outdoors. His stable also has to be mucked out, not merely for the physical reasons of general hygiene, but also for psychological ones as horses generally dislike being near their own excreta. Then there is also the necessity of providing regular and frequent food and checking rugs or blankets. Time and convenience are, therefore, important factors in caring for stabled horses.

The advantages of stabling a horse are that it is relatively easy to keep him clean as he will not have the opportunity to coat himself in mud. He will always be on hand when he is needed and he can also be kept fitter than a horse at grass (although a yarded horse can be just as fit), particularly as his diet can be controlled minutely, if necessary. This latter point may be important in horses whose work is physically demanding and who cannot perform at their optimum level if they are eating too much good grass.

To sum up, fully stabling horses is obviously extremely artificial, and even if a horse is exercised night and morning but has no 'playtime', it is not a system most modern, caring owners would choose. Just because it is traditional that does not make it acceptable. A horse kept in this way needs to be very placid and of an independent nature (few are). For a working owner, the system is extremely time-consuming due to the amount of exercise that must be given and the amount of mucking out that is needed, which also adds to cost because of expenditure on bedding.

Stabling horses full time is obviously extremely artificial, and even if a horse is exercised morning and night, he has no 'playtime'.

at grass

Horses evolved to live on grassland and in company. Time on pasture should make up a significant part of a horse's life.

SEEN BY MANY as the most natural system of horse keeping, the outdoor life does have disadvantages for both horse and owner. Some breeds usually do not thrive when out in cold, wet, windy weather, including Thoroughbreds and Arabs and other equines that originate in hot climates. Such thin-skinned animals are prone to suffer from exposure in winter as well as unbearable attacks by insects in summer. Other horses suffer badly from mud fever and rain rash (not necessarily in winter) and, despite shelter sheds and turnout rugs, simply cannot stand being out in a cold field. In summer, photosensitization is another problem, mainly in pink-skinned animals, and where there is no shade, relentless exposure to hot sun is mentally distressing and physically exhausting.

Outdoor horses can, of course, exercise themselves at will – although they tend not to do so when miserable but simply stand moping, pacing anxiously or even weaving or crib biting (if prone to these habits). They can eat grass and drink when they please (a suitable source permitting). When kept in groups, they can enjoy the company of their own kind and develop natural social relationships – something denied stabled animals and those (such as most stallions) that are kept in solitary conditions.

From their attendants' points of view, such horses are not quite as tying as stabled horses, although they should be visited twice daily to check on their general wellbeing, and so that early action can be taken in case of accidents, kicks and illness, and for feeding, if necessary. A certain amount of grooming should be done – at least discharges from eyes and nostrils should be assessed and sponged away, feet should be picked out and shoes, if worn, checked. Turnout rugs, when worn, should be adjusted and maybe changed twice daily.

Provided they are on grazing of fairly low nutritional content (although it must be clean and well cared for), grass-kept horses can be very fit, as proved by many endurance horses. Except in dry weather, they will not, certainly, be as clean as their stabled counterparts, which will not worry them but may worry their owners. In winter, they may well eat more food than stabled horses and it is certainly not so convenient to care for them outdoors in bad weather, unless they can be tied up temporarily in their shelter or somewhere under cover.

Horses kept at grass are not so time-consuming as others because the horse can exercise himself in the field, although he will need other work to maintain a level of fitness. You may worry, however, about exposure and wet ground in winter and insect attacks in summer. Really effective shelter is essential; you must be certain that other horses are not keeping yours from sheltering – the most common reason for horses not using shelter facilities, and often leading their owners to think that it is not needed because it is not used!

the combined system

THIS SYSTEM is a combination of stabling and turn out, and many authorities believe it to be the best way of keeping any horse. The system is very flexible, the number of hours in and out varying according to daily circumstances. Its advantages and disadvantages are simply those of the previous two systems but more moderate: in practice, the combined system works very well because the horse can have the freedom of an outdoor life but with the shelter of his stable when needed. He can be kept as fit as any stabled horse but because he can also be turned out he is not as tying as a fully stabled animal. Feed and bedding can be saved according to the time of year and the length of time out, although grazing may have to be rented. In general, this is probably the best system of all, apart from yarding with shelter and access to grass.

The combined system is ideal for avoiding the problems that might occur with the other systems: exposure and cold in winter and excess heat and insect attacks in summer with the outdoor system, and boredom, frustration and inner tension, resulting in various vices (stereotypies or abnormal behaviours) and other physical and psychological problems with full stabling. With stabled horses, these problems occur even when they are given what is considered to be adequate exercise – the traditional amount stated in most standard texts being two hours daily for a healthy, fairly fit horse.

A good and logical way to operate the combined management system is for the horse to be in at night and out during the day in winter, but in during the day and out at night in summer. In this way, you offer protection from the extremes of both seasons, always using your discretion about precise conditions on a daily basis. Contrary to popular opinion, provided they associate their stable with comfort and security, horses do like to come in quite often when conditions are not to their liking. They will readily let humans know about this by waiting at the gate to be brought in. Even having a field shelter available is not enough for some more sensitive types, and there is also the psychological aspect of wanting to be cared for and part of things.

In my experience, horses rarely appreciate extremes of either of the first two systems and because of its obvious practical advantages I am a great fan of the combined system.

Even a relatively small yard is better than nothing. This building, although not very big, is ample for three compatible horses that can come and go as they wish.

yarding and coralling

Spacious, well-ventilated yards like this can be made in any large, strong building. With the doors open, the horses can also have access outdoors, creating an ideal environment for them.

ANOTHER SYSTEM that is not used nearly enough in Britain or Ireland but is common in some other countries is yarding; it is suitable not only for breeding stock and resting horses but is also very good for horses in work.

The horses are kept in enclosures with some kind of cushioning and safe flooring – plain earth can be used, woodchips, woodshavings, straw, tan bark, sand and so on. The enclosures can be partly or fully roofed so the horses have the freedom to exercise themselves as much as space will allow but with the advantage of significant shelter. Sometimes the enclosure is a yard attached to a large, open-fronted shed or barn that is bedded down and the horses can come and go as they wish. In other cases, a single stable may have a smaller yard leading from it which simply permits the horse to walk about and have a measure of freedom, like the bull pens that were common in bygone days.

The system has much to recommend it because it gives horses some freedom without entailing the disadvantages of their being out at grass. Even with dirt yards, there will not normally be grass in any

quantity, so horses are fed as stabled horses. Basically, you can arrange your facilities any way you wish so long as the horses have shelter, space, freedom and company plus, of course, food and water. If the layout permits, it is ideal to have a surfaced yard leading out onto grass with a gate or sliprails dividing the two facilities. In this way, you can grant or deny your horses grass according to circumstances and requirements.

Corralling is closely allied to yarding, except that the horses do not normally have shelter, which can be a big disadvantage. They are kept in a high-fenced pen and fed as stabled horses but have the freedom to exercise themselves. The corral is also often used for training purposes, like a big round pen, whether from the ground or under saddle.

Yarding or corralling reduces the need to work your horse, but he will not take as much exercise as he would if he were on pasture. Also, there is the expense of having to provide forage because of the lack of grass. However, for horses who need their grazing limited from a health viewpoint, this can be good.

know your own horse

THE CHOICE OF a suitable system for you and your horse depends on several things. Most important of these is your horse's constitution and temperament. Neither of you will be happy if you choose the wrong method, and your horse's physical health and psychological wellbeing will probably suffer. As a caring owner, this will worry you and add to your stress levels. Other considerations are obviously your budget, your time constraints, and so on.

Horses and ponies of all types are fine living out in winter provided the conditions are not extreme and their basic needs are catered for.

understand his mental and physical needs and tendencies so that you can try to keep him in the most suitable way.

Breed and type are usually reliable indicators to how the horse needs to be kept *but not always*. There are many hot-blooded types that winter out happily given good facilities; likewise, just because cobs are regarded as placid (not all of them are), not particularly sensitive to the elements or given to wanting to be on the go all the time, it does not mean that all of them can live out with equanimity or, conversely, stay happily stabled most of the time on limited exercise. Thoroughbreds, as an extreme hot-blood type, are not always hot-headed, full of energy and super-sensitive to the weather.

Remember that unhappy horses do not thrive and they will cost more to keep than contented ones. Those who develop abnormal behaviour patterns, such as eating wood and droppings, pacing their stable or enclosure, head twirling, scraping their front teeth along the stable door or wall, kicking the walls or door, are showing clear signs of psychological and maybe physical distress. They often develop digestive troubles, which means that their food is not being properly utilized, and may be more or less permanently uncomfortable from indigestion or actual gut pain.

In selecting the right system, be guided mainly by your horse's needs. You may not have much choice over where you keep him, but it is better to have peace of mind by, for example, keeping your horse a little further from your home than you would wish but knowing that he is being accommodated according to his needs, than it is to have him nearby but forced to put up with conditions that make him unhappy and worry you. It is essential to really be honest with yourself about what kind of character your horse has, and to

THINK
PROPER MANAGEMENT

It is scientifically proven that most horses who are fed a high-concentrate, low-fibre diet and spend more time in than out will have gastric ulcers. Although there are feed additives that can control this, they are not the moral or aesthetic answer in my opinion. The solution is to manage the horse properly – provide more freedom, fewer concentrates and more fibre (see pp.114–119).

at home

Keeping your horse at home may seem the ideal solution for you and your horses' needs but most horses are not happy on their own. You can ensure he has company by catering for more than one horse.

FOR MANY OWNERS this is the best way to keep a horse. It is much more convenient than having to travel to your horse, you can normally be sure that no one is tampering with him and because you and your family or friends look after him yourselves, you can be fairly certain that he is cared for according to his and your requirements. However, if you are keeping your horse at home and doing him entirely yourself with no help, it is extremely tying unless you can get occasional help for when you are ill or away.

facilities

The main problem with keeping your horse at home in many areas is getting permission to erect horse facilities if they don't already exist. In Britain, temporary buildings are increasingly popular as they do not normally need planning permission. Purpose-built shelters on wheels or skids are available, or you can construct a strong, neat-looking shelter out of straw bales, polythene or felted wooden roofing and strong wooden supports to lash everything to. Laws and regulations vary

greatly and your best plan is to ask other 'at home' owners for advice, not to mention a legal expert, to try to assess difficulties before going ahead.

Even taking into account the expense of providing facilities at home, your costs will be less than keeping the horse elsewhere because you will have no rent or livery charges and, of course, the stables and ancillary buildings will add to the value of your property. However, they will also increase your insurance and local taxes costs. In residential areas you will need to give serious thought to the positioning and disposal of your muck heap in order to avoid complaints from neighbours. Many owners give away muck – just putting a notice at the gate inviting people to help themselves to it. Your local council may take it for parks and gardens, too.

From your horse's point of view, the main disadvantages of being at home may be lack of turn out space and company. Giving him plenty of exercise and having a space big enough for him to kick up his heels and have a good roll may be enough, and perhaps you can rent grazing nearby. The company issue may be solved by a small pony (watch out for laminitis), although this will increase your responsibilities and the time it takes to care for your horses, or by having a (helpful) friend stable their horse with you free of charge, which, if it works well, may help you save time as you can share jobs.

YOU WILL HAVE TO CONSIDER

- *Awkward neighbours*
- *Access for delivery wagons, for the fire service and other vehicles*
- *Disposal of manure in urban areas*
- *Drainage and smells*
- *Restrictions on storage of inflammable materials, such as feed and bedding*
- *Horse-proof fencing*
- *Secure storage for valuable items*
- *Water and electricity supplies*

which system?

at livery

TIME IS MONEY and it is sometimes necessary to spend one in order to save the other. With livery arrangements, you are spending money to save time because, in theory, if you are paying full livery fees someone else is doing the work and there should never be any *need* for you to go and see your horse. You go because you *want* to spend time with him.

The main complaints from livery clients are that (a) stable proprietors simply do not provide the facilities or services for which they are paying and (b) stable proprietors place unreasonable restrictions on how horses may be looked after, often disregarding their needs.

A professionally-run yard will offer a livery contract (see p.19); peruse this *very* closely to discover ambiguously worded or unduly restrictive clauses that enable the proprietor to get out of almost anything and also allow them to 'move the goalposts' without warning, usually to the detriment of horses and clients. 'Turn out', for instance, may not mean onto grass so clarify this. And your horse's times out and even his companions may be very restricted. Many yards in Britain do not offer winter turn out at all or offer only very short periods on a surfaced area – unforgivable, in my view.

In addition, you may be tied to buying your feed and bedding from the proprietor, who may not be willing to get the brands or types you want. You may not be able to have the trainer, farrier or even vet of your choice. You may not be able to feed your horse yourself, have your friends down to ride him, work him loose in the arena or even be at the stables at times to suit you.

If you do find a suitable yard, have a Plan A (an alternative yard to go to), and ideally Plans B and C. Keep a folder with livery adverts and phone numbers and keep your eye on the market to see what else is available in your area, in case your current yard becomes unbearable due to unpleasant proprietors, yard politics or abuse of your horse.

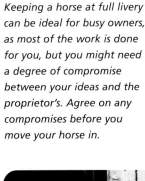

Keeping a horse at full livery can be ideal for busy owners, as most of the work is done for you, but you might need a degree of compromise between your ideas and the proprietor's. Agree on any compromises before you move your horse in.

Two fairly typical livery problems:

 Pat took her horse to an apparently ideal livery yard, making it clear to the proprietor that she worked semi-professionally as a trainer. She usually worked freelance on other owners' premises but on one occasion obtained permission to bring a client's horse from some distance away to the yard. Its owner paid the livery charge to the proprietor and paid Pat for training.

After two weeks, the behaviour of Pat's own horse deteriorated; he resumed a biting and kicking propensity and his former weaving habit. It was found that another horse owner there, an unofficial yard manager and trainer (with the proprietor's consent) was abusing the horse and also lying about Pat's abilities, in an effort to take Pat's clients. Pat reported matters to the proprietor who simply said there would be no hard feelings if she left, refusing to do anything about the unofficial manager, who later turned out to be his mistress. Pat is now back at her previous yard – not a satisfactory outcome. The moral of this story is that you often cannot do anything about yard politics. Reporting difficulties to the yard owner or manager may result in abuse of your horse, which you will not wish to risk. If the yard proprietor himself or herself is the miscreant, you have no option but to leave.

2 *After several incidents of abuse of her horse and theft of her feed, bedding and equipment, Margaret made discreet enquiries among other owners at her superb livery yard, and was not surprised to discover that two women who were jealous of her competition successes were the culprits.*

The proprietor refused to discuss the matter on the grounds of lack of evidence (the other owners didn't want to become involved) so Margaret moved her horse to a rather run-down and very casually run DIY stables, initally on a temporary basis. She and the horse are so happy there that they have stayed. The moral of this story is that the physical appearance of the yard is often not important, provided it is safe. What matters is the attitude of the other people on the yard, particularly the proprietor or manager but also the other owners. In any livery situation, you cannot judge these until you have 'lived' there a while. This is why it is so important to keep an up-to-date list of several other places you could go to if things become unacceptable.

where to keep your horse

livery choices

full livery There are various concepts of full livery, but these days it usually means that the horse's basic needs are met. He will probably be brushed over, fed, watered, mucked out, rugs attended to, turned out and brought in as part of the deal, but jobs such as tack cleaning, ridden exercise, full grooming, washing rugs and so on will be charged extra, as, of course, will training, show or hunting preparation, clipping and trimming, but at least you know they are available should you need them. All owners expect to pay their own farriery and veterinary fees. The yard should have its own professional indemnity insurance but owners need their own third-party and veterinary insurances.

Sometimes the fees can be reduced by having your horse on working livery, which means that he will be ridden by students and other clients. This may work if you stipulate that only competent riders may ride him, otherwise his standard of performance and his mental attitude may deteriorate. A disadvantage of working livery is that he may not be available when you want him.

part/half livery This is cheaper than full livery because you get fewer services. Most half livery clients choose to have their horse done for them in the mornings (fed, watered, rugs seen to, turned out and maybe mucked out) so that their early mornings are less of a mad rush and they only need to go to the stables in the evenings and at weekends. This suits many busy owners as there are opportunities to pay for extras, such as care over a weekend, or bringing your horse in when you are working late, if necessary.

do-it-yourself livery This means that you pay the stable proprietor rent for a stable and grazing or other turn out facilities when the ground is bad, and the use of any riding areas (prepared arena, jumping field). You usually also pay them for hay or haylage; some yards include bedding but not normally concentrates or bucket feeds. There are normally no services provided except under such circumstances as illness or holidays, and even then most owners depend on friends to care for their horse.

The problem with DIY livery is that many proprietors simply want the rent: they are not interested in yard politics, friendships or enmities, controlling the muck heap, the state of the yard or even, in many cases,

Do-it-yourself livery is the most common option for many owners as it is the cheapest and you have complete control (facilities and the co-operation of the proprietor granted) over your horse's management.

the state of the horses, and the latter can be a significant problem, especially as many owners are loath to report cruelty cases for fear of recriminations on their own horses. In addition, even in a good DIY yard, you will have to meet most of your horse's needs yourself, which will mean plenty of early mornings and late nights, and careful planning when you want an evening out or a holiday.

If you opt for a DIY yard, it is strongly advised that you choose a well managed

yard that has good security and safety systems in place; it should also have an interested and knowledgeable proprietor or manager who is prepared to oversee owners' behaviour and keep an eye on the horses' wellbeing. This person will need to be willing to intervene in any arguments, such as grazing groups and companions, and should be prepared to arrange for someone to tend a horse whose owner does not show up for whatever reason. They should generally run a tidy and humane set-up.

where to keep your horse

assessing a yard

CHOOSING A LIVERY YARD can be quite difficult from the point of view of finding one that will give you and your horse peace of mind, but assessing the quality of a yard is fairly easy – you simply use as your main guideline the mental and physical condition of the horses that are already there.

If you have any feel for horses at all, you should be able to tell whether or not they are happy, interested and comfortable, up tight or downright miserable, whether they are in good bodily condition, too fat or too thin, whether the stables show signs of excessive wood chewing, whether the grazing paddocks are littered with droppings (and other things), whether the water supply is adequate and clean and whether the horses and their surroundings are reasonably clean and looking well cared for. (Precise details of management topics are given in 'Care In A Nutshell', which starts on p.100.)

Just as important, of course, is whether you get a feeling, deep down, that you can at least get on with the proprietor or manager and grooms (if applicable). Try to get some idea of what kind of people the other owners are and whether or not you feel you could get on with them, too. Not always easy!

Finally, when choosing a yard, the location should be considered carefully. If you want to spend your time hacking rather than riding in a school, for instance, it is no use keeping your horse at a place surrounded by dangerous roads. Or if you wish to improve your and your horse's prowess across country, for example, it will be inconvenient if there is no facility for cross-country riding, either on the premises or nearby.

TWENTY QUESTIONS TO ASK A YARD OWNER

- *Which would be my horse's stable?*
- *What are the grazing/turn out arrangements year-round?*
- *Who is in charge of the establishment should there be any problems or queries?*
- *Are there any restrictions on when I may come to see my horse?*
- *May I feed and look after my own horse, even if he is on full livery?*
- *May I use a trainer, farrier and veterinary practice of my choice?*
- *Would I have to buy my supplies and equipment from you?*
- *May I buy the brands/types of feed, bedding and medical supplies I want?*
- *Which would be my tack/equipment area?*
- *What are your security arrangements?*
- *What are your safety arrangements, including location of fire extinguishers and so on?*
- *What steps would you take in the event of abuse of a horse or theft of property?*
- *Who would call the vet if my horse became ill or injured and I could not be contacted?*
- *What are your insurance arrangements?*
- *Do you offer a legally binding livery contract?*
- *Are you and your staff qualified and experienced?*
- *Would students be handling my horse? If yes, would this be under supervision?*
- *Are there any restrictions on the use of the training/riding facilities?*
- *Is there good hacking nearby with safe access or are there busy roads to negotiate?*
- *In the event of frozen or baked ground, do you allow the use of used bedding (muck) to create riding or lungeing tracks or would the horses be confined to their stables?*

SAMPLE LIVERY CONTRACT

There are many versions of livery contracts. This is a partially filled example.

This contract is between Joan Smith trading as Trapalanda Livery Stables at Green Lane, Belltown (hereinafter referred to as The Proprietor) and Shirley Andrews (hereinafter referred to as The Owner) and is dated this _____ day of _____ 20**.

1) The Proprietor undertakes the care of the 9-year-old chestnut Warmblood gelding Danny Boy who is the property of Shirley Andrews of 92 York Road, Singleton and will take all reasonable care of and responsibility for the above horse, while in her care.

2) The agreed fee for part-livery as detailed on the attached sheet will be _____ per month, payable in advance. The Proprietor will inform The Owner three months in advance of any change in livery fees or one week in advance of any change in services.

3) Should the owner wish to terminate this agreement, one month's notice in writing will be required, or the payment of one month's fee in lieu.

4) The Proprietor may terminate this agreement by giving the owner one month's notice in writing.

5) In the event of non-payment of livery fees, interest will be charged at 25 per cent of the amount outstanding and appropriate legal action taken to ensure recovery of outstanding monies.

6) The Owner is responsible for all veterinary and farriery fees.

7) The stables are open for The Owner to visit between 8am and 9pm on weekdays and between 8am and 6pm at weekends, except by prior arrangement in the event of competition days, sickness of the horse, etc.

8) The Owner will ensure that at all times adequate supplies of feed, bedding and equipment are available for the horse's care.

9) The Owner agrees that The Proprietor may call a veterinary practice of her choosing should Danny Boy become sick or injured and The Owner cannot be contacted, that she may take whatever action she considers necessary for the welfare of Danny Boy and that The Owner will pay all expenses connected therewith.

10) The Owner will leave with The Proprietor all telephone numbers for herself, her farrier and her veterinary practice.

11) Danny Boy is required to be de-wormed according to The Proprietor's existing programme which may be changed at any time on veterinary advice. The Proprietor will administer the requisite drugs and charge The Owner accordingly.

12) Danny Boy is required to be vaccinated against the following diseases:_____ _____. The Owner will ensure that these vaccinations are kept up-to-date as evidenced by valid vaccination certificates which will be lodged with the Proprietor.

13) The indoor school, outdoor arena, jumping field and cross-country course are available free of charge for riding and schooling but a charge of _____ per hour will be made for lessons using these facilities from visiting trainers.

14) The Owner will not feed her horse at other than the set feeding times of 7am, 12 noon and 5pm although hay and haylage may be given.

15) Danny Boy will be turned out to graze every day except in circumstances such as exceptionally bad ground conditions as judged by The Proprietor, extreme weather conditions or in the event of his sickness or injury according to veterinary advice. When the grazing paddocks are unsuitable because of weather conditions or land management treatments, Danny Boy will be provided with exercise at liberty on the surfaced riding arena with appropriate company.

16) The Owner will not use the facilities at Trapalanda Livery Stables for any commercial enterprise such as teaching or training without the prior agreement of The Proprietor.

17) All matters concerning the management of the business and the facilities and services provided are under the sole control of The Proprietor and although all reasonable steps will be taken to inform The Owner of any changes in the administration of the business which may affect her and Danny Boy, The Proprietor reserves the right to alter facilities and services as she deems necessary.

Signed_____   Signed _____
      The Proprietor   The Owner

Dated _____   Dated _____

where to keep your horse

other ideas

YOU MAY BE ABLE to have your horse cared for and accommodated free, or for the cost of feed and bedding, if he acts as companion to another horse. Many owners who manage alone would welcome part-time help, too, and you could come to a mutual agreement over stable work to the benefit of you and your horse.

There can be problems, though, when you are keeping your horse at a private home, whatever the specific agreement, as opposed to in a yard that is run as a business. One of the main problems is when the owner considers that they are doing you a favour, even when you are paying good money or that you are made to feel awkward visiting at odd times of the day. Many such people (whose favourite phrase is 'but this is my home, not a business') are willing to take your money, not declare it to the tax authorities, and treat your horse like a third-rate citizen who comes firmly and regularly at the bottom of the heap. My experience is that you are far better to have a proper business arrangement in a professional, insured yard with competent but caring staff – and have a proper livery contract setting out everything from both points of view.

You may be lucky enough to find premises rent free, in return for you undertaking to put and keep them in good repair although, again, a written agreement is essential if you want to avoid the risk of eviction as soon as the repairs are complete. 'Gentlemen's agreements' have a habit of quickly becoming most ungentlemanlike.

If you are the entrepreneurial type, you could rent a yard and then charge others rent, not only covering your costs but making a profit as well, particularly if you can act as manager. As this would certainly be construed as a business by the local council, you must check that it will be allowed on those particular premises. Also, if you take on such a project, you must be sure that you have the time, personality and expertise to run it properly, otherwise you will find your clients will become unhappy and unco-operative.

1 Fully assess your own lifestyle and your horse's psychological and physical propensities and needs before deciding on a management system to suit you both. Neither of you will be happy if you get it wrong.

2 If you keep your horse at home, make sure local regulations allow you to do this, particularly if you have to build facilities. It would be tragic to have to dismantle your dream.

3 When considering livery, remember that time is money and you often have to spend one to save the other. It is far better, for example, to keep your horse at a slightly more expensive but top quality yard a little further from your home than you would wish, than it is to go for a cheaper yard with poorer facilities and unreliable services because it is just round the corner.

4 It is crucial to be able to rely on and trust the other people involved in your horse's care, otherwise your life will be a constant nightmare of worrying and wondering – and so will your horse's.

5 When assessing a potential livery stable for your horse, remember that the state of the horses is far more important than a slightly untidy yard, peeling paintwork or minor repairs waiting to be done.

6 Especially on DIY yards, find out just who is responsible for the maintenance of the facilities and the provision of the services – you are paying for both. All too often, there is no one responsible for or interested in anything other than taking the money.

7 Always have a Plan A and, ideally, Plans B and C. In other words, have phone numbers and addresses of other livery yards or places where you could keep your horse, even temporarily, should your present yard become absolutely impossible.

8 In the case of significant neglect of a horse, pony or any other animal on your yard, remember that you can safely report it to a relevant animal charity or the police because it is invariably their policy not to reveal the identity of their informants to avoid recriminations, and they should assure you of this.

2

Your Horse Year

The equestrian year never stops but simply turns full circle; while some equestrian disciplines have their seasons, others continue through the year and are only divided into an indoor season, normally in winter, and an outdoor season, normally in summer. For the owner of the general-purpose horse, there are more than enough equestrian activities to take part in to keep you occupied all year round.

In the midst of your horsey activities, there will be times when you don't feel like riding or can't, for some reason. All sorts of things happen to disrupt your riding. There are planned things such as family holidays, weekends or days out with your friends, and periods when other events take over such as exams or a particularly busy time at work.

Then there are unplanned things such as injury or sickness involving you, your family or your animals, unexpected extremes of weather (especially in Britain, where we often get all four seasons in one day!), disease epidemics, which put normal regional or even national activities on indefinite hold – and, of course, simply not being in the mood.

Whatever your inclinations, you have a whole year, every year, in which to plan for and enjoy your horse as you wish.

winter

WINTER IS THE WORST time of year for most horse owners. Whenever they occur, extremes of weather are never welcomed by either horses or humans, but winter also has short days and long nights, making life particularly difficult. The lack of daylight cuts down on riding time, reduces the time you have to check fences and do maintenance work, and on some yards severely limits your horse's turn out. In addition, in some regions winter can be a miserable, wet, bone-chilling time rather than an invigorating, crisp enjoyable one.

In still, dry winter weather, unclipped animals really do not need rugs unless they are truly very fine-skinned.

exercising If you are lucky enough to have access to a large American barn-type facility or some kind of indoor complex, there will probably be indoor loose boxes, maybe with an indoor exercise track or shedrow around its perimeter, and/or at least one covered riding arena. All these will make your life much easier as you can give your horse some effective exercise in a relatively short time. If you don't have such luxuries, you'll have no choice but to exercise out-of-doors and here your farrier will be able to help with frost nails, ice studs or shoes designed especially for winter conditions.

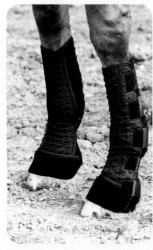

Special boots or 'equichaps' can be very effective in protecting your horse's legs from mud fever in wet conditions.

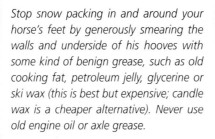

AVOID 'SNOWBALLS'

Stop snow packing in and around your horse's feet by generously smearing the walls and underside of his hooves with some kind of benign grease, such as old cooking fat, petroleum jelly, glycerine or ski wax (this is best but expensive; candle wax is a cheaper alternative). Never use old engine oil or axle grease.

weather protection You can now get special boots to protect legs from the effects of sharp ice and mud. With some sensitive horses even one exposure to mud can result in a bad case of mud fever (scratches). Clay soils are the worst for this, and soils with synthetic

IS HE COLD OR NOT?

To tell if your horse is cold and needs a rug or blanket, place the flat of your bare hand on his belly, flanks, loins and quarters and around the base of his ears, allowing time for heat to come through any long hair. If these areas feel cold, your horse is cold, but if they're warm, so is he. Obvious signs such as shivering, hair standing on end, tight skin and an anxious or distressed look about his face and ears are also clear indications that he feels cold. If your horse is relaxed and warm, he doesn't need rugging.

fertilizers or pesticides can cause bad reactions in some animals. In average muddy conditions, you can protect your horse against problems by smearing liquid paraffin or mineral oil onto *clean, dry* legs, putting it on upwards against the lie of the hair so that it reaches the skin. This is thin enough to rinse off easily and quickly on a daily basis so you can get the legs properly clean and dry before reapplying it.

A hand-held hairdryer can be useful for drying legs – and certainly speeds up the job – or try wrapping the legs with loose-knit or permeable fabric bandages or wraps to dry off while you do other jobs.

Sadly, many owners over-clip and then over-rug, making their horse's life worse, through overheating, weight, pressure and skin irritation. Using too much clothing on your horse also increases your work load, not only because you have to keep putting it on and taking it off but also because you have to keep it clean and decent to wear. Save time and effort by having two rugs of each type.

While over-rugging is not recommended, no rugs at all may result in horses and ponies of any type getting hypothermia or at least very chilly, which may lead to loss of condition and real misery, so don't be tempted to avoid rugging altogether, even if your horses are well fed – be guided by your horse. Decent shelter with a dry floor area should also be a basic essential.

feed for warmth
The most effective way to keep horses warm is to provide them with a constant supply of fibre as hay, haylage or branded forage feeds. Fibre is mainly digested low down the digestive tract and produces slow-release, long-term warmth and energy, whereas concentrates (sweet feeds) are digested higher up the tract and produce swift boosts of energy that soon run out, leaving the horse feeling hungry and cold again. Concentrates may be needed as a back-up or a top-up and are necessary for hard-working horses (see pp.108–119).

spring

SPRING'S MILDER WEATHER is a relief to most of us. The flies haven't become bothersome (although early protection against midges will be needed for sensitive horses) but one serious disadvantage is the possibility of too much spring grass triggering laminitis in susceptible individuals, so grazing will have to be rationed (see also Autumn, p.27). It is safer to turn horses out during darkness when sugar levels in the grass have fallen. If not gradually introduced to spring grass after a winter without grazing, some animals can also develop colic. Colic and laminitis, or founder, are both very painful, incapacitating and potentially fatal. On the other hand, if the grass is of poor to medium quality and the horse is used to having grass before being turned out fully, long spring days out in the field while you are at work can be very pleasant for him

and labour- and cost-saving for you – less mucking out, grooming and exercising. Make the most of it.

exercise and care
Longer daylight hours make exercising your horse safer and more pleasant, although it can still be pretty cold in early spring so don't be in too much of a hurry to put away night-time rugs or blankets. The weather can also backtrack suddenly, so turnout rugs and shelter will still be needed. Rugs and shelter are particularly important for a horse being roughed off and turned away for a break after a winter season, particularly if he is fit, with no spare fat, and has been clipped, stabled and fed concentrates. Such horses suffer greatly when thoughtlessly turned out without proper protection and care. It certainly saves time, effort and money because you don't have a time-consuming, expensively stabled horse on your hands, but you could lose him from hypothermia – no exaggeration.

If your horse has been out all winter, spring could be the time when his season starts again, with a veterinary check, shoeing, worming, vaccinations and a gradual start to his fitness programme. He will probably have been fed both hay/haylage and concentrates while out so should have no digestive problems due to a changeover.

INTERNAL PARASITES

Spring often sees a surge in the populations of worms, so pay particular attention to your worm-egg checks and treatment. Although it is very time-consuming, picking up droppings from grazing land is the best way to prevent infestation. Alternatively, if you have plenty of space, practise paddock rotation; cross-grazing with cows and/or sheep can also reduce worm populations.

summer

Mesh fly and midge sheets mean that many animals that are prone to sweet itch and who would otherwise not be able to be turned out can live a much more comfortable life.

THE ADVANTAGES OF summer include warmer temperatures (other than extremes), no need to rug up and dry the horse if he is wet, unless the weather is really unseasonal, no bulky clothes for us and, of course, lovely long evenings and light mornings which altogether make horse management so much easier and more pleasant. While the weather is dry, make plans for winter, too. Get your rugs repaired and cleaned – avoid the autumn rush – and think about how you can make life easier for yourself perhaps by arranging your stabling and grazing differently. What were your main problems last winter, and how can you avoid them next time?

flies This season can, however, be as miserable for the horse as winter. First, there are the major problems caused by flies. Most owners do not realize, and some simply ignore, the very real torture horses can go through when they are exposed to insects. It is worse during the daylight hours, but there are night-flying insects that bother horses, too.

Although nature does equip a horse with various anti-fly devices such as manes, tails and forelocks and extensive flat muscling under the skin of the back, sides and flanks so he can twitch flies off those areas, to keep himself permanently free from them he must keep up a non-stop performance of head-shaking, leg-stamping, muscle-twitching and tail-swishing which is mentally and physically wearying. In bad cases, insects drive horses to stampede around their paddocks, which is exhausting and damaging, particularly in the case of unfit animals. Legs become badly jarred and feet bruised, chipped and cracked.

Sweet itch is a particularly distressing spring and summer condition suffered by horses allergic to the saliva of the culicoides midge, which is active around sunrise and sunset. As treatment of established sweet itch is still difficult and very inconvenient, the best method of dealing with it is prevention (see p.133). This applies to all insect attacks.

hyperthermia
Another major problem in what we humans call a 'good' summer is hyperthermia. This is caused by the sun and heat and is where the body warms up to dangerous temperatures. Shelter areas are as vital now as in winter – this time for their cool shade.

autumn

Autumn is often a very pleasant time to be turned out – but, as always, there are potential dangers. Acorns and conkers, for instance, can be poisonous, and the autumn flush of grass can result in laminitis.

AUTUMN BRINGS A RETURN to kinder conditions for horses. There are no extremes of heat or sun, flies gradually disappear and the ground softens. The grass gives an autumn flush of growth, too, but it is of low protein content so if your horse is relying on grass for food at this time of year, a protein supplement may be needed – take the advice of a nutritionist or a vet who is interested in nutrition.

avoiding laminitis As good autumn grass is high in carbohydrates, you may need to restrict the grazing of animals prone to obesity or laminitis, as in spring. Autumn laminitis takes many owners unaware and they are totally puzzled when their horse or pony shows clear symptoms of the disease. The treatment, as always, is to follow veterinary advice and to bed the animal on deep, soft, dry bedding with rationed hay and fibre feeds plus supplements for the maintenance of the feet – as all this is costly in terms of time and money, as well as extra work for you, to say nothing of not being able to ride and your horse's extreme discomfort, it is best to be extremely careful over grazing, particularly in the mornings after a cold or frosty night, when the grass is at its most dangerous.

Many feed companies produce special feeds for laminitics with easily recognizable logos on the sacks. In addition, most good firms have helplines offering reliable feeding information, so it's easy to get up-to-date advice. Forget the old ideas of starving laminitics: this has been known to be wrong for at least 15 years yet so many people still do it. *A restricted diet with specific nutrients is what is needed, plus frog supports or heart-bar shoes and REST – no walking.*

FOG

Nights start to draw in, in the autumn, so blankets could be needed, at least overnight. Autumn fog often brings its own problems. Although it might be possible to exercise a horse at dusk or in the dark if you are wearing high-visibility gear and have efficient lighting, only an imbecile would purposely take a horse out on a public highway in fog, even if it is lit up like a Christmas tree, so other means of exercising must be devised.

considering fitness

your big advantage

WHATEVER WORK your horse is to do (because it is still all work to him, even if it is pleasure to you), he has to be made fit and to be cared for appropriately for the discipline concerned. To make the most of this book, you need to have a reasonable standard of knowledge on keeping horses (read Care in a Nutshell, pp.100–140, to brush up on any vague areas). This section deals with the different aspects of each season of the year and how they affect preparation for various disciplines.

It takes much less time and effort to keep a horse fit than to get him fit. An all-round, family-type or riding/saddle club horse will probably be in work most of the year and will, therefore, usually be about half- to three-quarters fit (taking fully fit to mean racing, three-day eventing or endurance-race fit). This is a considerable advantage to both owner and horse because this type of fitness will be quite adequate for what you want your horse to do and can be maintained by his normal work plus a bit extra. It is also better for his general health to be always partially fit like this than to be allowed to get fat and soft in summer or thin, weather-beaten and run-down in winter.

fit – unfit? To restore a horse to reasonable fitness from being either fat and soft, or thin and run-down needs a lot of time, slow work, patience and skill in feeding and judgement of his changing physical and mental condition. Without these qualities in the owner or carer, it is easy to over-stress an unfit horse so that he ends up with legs that won't withstand the season you want to ride him in because they weren't given enough slow roadwork, for instance, at the beginning of a fitness programme, or slight heart strain because fast work, even short pipe-openers, was begun too soon or carried on too long.

Generally speaking, a horse who is fairly fit and in work most of the year is less of a liability to his owner than one whose condition varies significantly with the seasons. The fairly fit horse is less susceptible to stresses and strains during the normal course of his work, healthier (provided his general care is correct and appropriate) and less prone to work-related injuries and even to accidents in the field. Because his body is tuned up, he can use it better to get out of difficulties, such as uneven ground or a tree that suddenly looms up and needs dodging, a mistake over a jump or a companion who decides to have a mad half hour and harass everybody else in the paddock.

Of course, you should also make the effort to acquire as much knowledge as you can so that you can manage your horse or horses under all conditions and in all states of wellbeing.

schedule planning

Keen competitors won't care about a downpour! There are enough activities – competitive and non-competitive – to keep any horse and owner busy throughout the year.

SIT DOWN WITH a year planner and plot out your year. First put in major events and your holidays, then put in the times of routine medicals, vaccinations, teeth checks, blood tests, worming treatments and anything else. Plan these to take place well before any events as some horses may need a little while to get over them or time may be required for results to be assessed and further action taken. Now factor in the time needed to prepare and condition your horse for what you want him to do – the basics for any equestrian activity are pretty much the same for the first six weeks or so (see p.32 for details relating to specific disciplines).

Now, you should have a clear picture of the horse's changing work pattern and,

therefore, of your own. By giving careful thought to his constitution and temperament (which have an important bearing on his management, see below) and to your own working times on a daily and yearly basis, plus the various equestrian activities you wish to take part in, you will be able to plan your year to best advantage, see quickly what is going to be involved in terms of time and expenditure during each season and organize yourself accordingly. (See also Your Budget, pp.39–41.)

be flexible

Ideally, your management method should be flexible enough to be altered according to your horse's work. In winter, if he is going to be turned out from Monday to Friday and only hacking at weekends, he probably won't need much clipping; he'll be able to withstand long days in the field better if he has more of his natural coat and a lighter rug or blanket, along with fewer concentrates. However, if you plan to hunt on Saturdays and work your horse a few times in the week to maintain his fitness, he will need some kind of clip and will be best brought in at night. As well as being more pleasant for a hard-working horse, clipping will reduce grooming time and enable you to dry him off more quickly if he does sweat. However, you will need to use warmer rugs when he is turned out and provide more feed.

In summer, your horse may need to be quite fit for strenuous weekends and evening hacks or lessons, but if your grazing is fairly rich, he will need to be in for at least part of his time to reduce his grass intake. Although stabling during the day may increase your workload, it is infinitely kinder to your horse than leaving him in the hot sun, where he will be bothered by flies and heat (see also p.10) – also it will save you time if you want to ride at the end of the day as he will be in waiting for you when you arrive at the yard. You could even groom him in the morning when you bring him in, thereby giving yourself a head start in the evening.

getting fit

preparing a sensible regime

COUNT BACKWARDS from your first outing of the year, assessing its type and the level of fitness required and therefore the number of weeks needed to achieve that, then put the start of the fitness programme on your planner. If your horse needs half-fitness, say, work back six weeks and mark this date to start, although adding an extra week or so for mishaps is a good idea.

In autumn or winter, it may be easier to get your horse fit if he is partly clipped and wears a turnout rug, depending on how thick his coat grows. In spring and summer, grass may have to be gradually restricted to produce a slimmer shape and allow for harder food to be fed for increasing work. Horses who do not follow the old-fashioned regime of being brought in completely, do get fit quicker as they exercise in their field more as they feel fitter and more active. Also, once fairly fit, you can reduce your walking periods slightly with them as they will be walking about more when at liberty.

walking The walking stage of a fitness programme should be at least two weeks and up to four. Animals aimed at pursuits where hard muscled-up fitness is not needed – say Riding Club work, showing, dressage, private driving and hacking – can be safely given two weeks. For those expected to do strenuous work such as eventing, polo, racing, higher levels of show-jumping, driving trials and endurance work, you will need to allow a month of walking building up to about two hours a day (with maybe one day a week off). During this work, you should get your horse to walk properly up to his bridle most of the time, but also allow for periods of relaxation.

The key to fitness and maintaining soundness, particularly leg soundness, is adequate preparation in the initial, walking stages of a fitness programme. Don't be tempted to rush your programme. If you skimp, you might as well not bother at all.

Trotting carefully on roads and tracks is an important part of the fitness programme. These two horses would gain even more benefit if their riders asked them to go with their heads and necks a little more down and out and their backs up.

A CUT-PRICE MANEGE

There's no doubt that a decent schooling area is a massive help for most disciplines.

A surfaced manège:

(You don't need a troublesome, expensive membrane with this method.)

- *Choose the driest spot in your paddocks – measure out the area you want to use, marking the corners with posts, and making sure you get them square*

- *Excavate it to a depth of at least 40cm (16in)*

- *Hand-lay a level layer of bricks or (cheaper) half-bricks on their sides on the bottom, each 1cm (½in) apart for drainage. This labour-intensive chore can be shared by friends, family and anyone who will want to use your manège and is truly the best foundation in my experience*

- *Ram or roll the brick layer carefully to level it further without cracking the bricks*

- *Brush over a layer of fine gravel to fill in the spaces*

- *Add a layer of smooth stones – 10cm (4in) deep*

- *Add a layer of coarser but not sharp gravel, such as river gravel – 10cm (4in) deep*

- *Finally, lay your chosen surface – 10cm (4in) deep*

A grass manège:

(This method should not require planning or attract any sort of tax or extra rates because you are not constructing anything, but do check with your local planning office first.)

- *On well-drained land, excavation is not essential, but if necessary, have your paddock drained*

- *When it has recovered, mow the grass short*

- *Measure out an area of your chosen size*

- *Lay a thin layer of sharp sand over the area and oversow it with hard-wearing, sports-pitch grasses, following the propagation instructions*

- *Keep the area spiked, mown and rolled throughout the growing season and you will have an arena that is useable for most of the year*

Remember: Horses evolved to go on grassland.

You can buy low, plastic, portable arenas with markers. Set these up to mark out both types of manège. On grass, consider allocating an area big enough for two manèges; this way you can move your markers around within your site to prevent excessive wear on tracks.

You can combine the two methods above. Excavate the area and lay the bricks, stones and gravel, then fill in with topsoil on which you can either sow suitable seed or lay sports-field turf. The finished area will look just like the grass manège but will be better drained.

trotting When trotting is introduced, it should be no more than a working trot, with your horse nicely in hand. You can start trotting on softer tracks and progress to harder ground but always keep it steady and rhythmical. If your horse is active, allow him to trot on a little rather than nag at him to keep him slow and maybe risk spoiling his urge to give you free, forward movement. (See p.139 for continuing a fitness programme; here you will find information about introducing canter work. Pay full attention to sensible feeding as your horse's work increases, too, pp.106–120.)

When you start your fitness regime, you can save time, effort and money by:

- Beginning work from the field for a week or two before stabling your horse

- Giving a very small concentrate feed on return from work, unless he is too fat, before turning him out

- Not shoeing him at first as long as he does his initial walking work in his field or on soft tracks. Short trips on hard, smooth roads should not harm him if his feet are of good conformation and horn quality and are correctly trimmed and balanced

getting fit

specializing

Show-jumpers need specific gymnastic schooling to develop the appropriate muscles for jumping.

THE FURTHER CONDITIONING of your horse depends on his discipline – remember to use your year planner to plot out the time required. You can do a lot of useful schooling while out riding, provided you don't sicken your horse by constantly nagging him. Bend round trees, jump fallen tree trunks, ditches and hedges, use uneven ground to develop balance and so on.

Endurance horses take up most time as long rides must become part of the routine to develop their stamina and accustom them to bearing weight for long periods of time.

Racehorses of various categories will need short canters with the length, speed and frequency of the workouts increasing until the horse is ready to race. His first race will also bring him on in fitness.

Event horses need to start specific dressage schooling and athletic jumping as well as long canters to build up stamina. They, too, need accustoming to covering distances relevant to their competitive demands. Many eventers are conditioned further (after the slow work) by interval training.

Show-jumpers, show horses and dressage horses need correct flatwork to build up their muscles, develop obedience and develop their agility and gymnastic prowess. Jumpers also need athletic jumping practice, like the eventers. Combine such work with rides out and hacks with schooling to avoid your horse getting bored.

DON'T FORGET YOURSELF

While you are building up your horse, you will also be increasing your own level of fitness, unless someone else is doing some of the work. Depending on your discipline, it may also be useful to do some exercising on your own, such as running, suppling work and swimming to improve your overall fitness and flexibility and make sure that you don't let your horse down. Factor all this in to your timetable – and budget.

TRAINING TIMELINE

This timeline assumes a fitness programme starting with an unfit, mature horse. It also assumes that you are familiar with the precise demands of your discipline and that you can judge your horse's capabilities and allow for his reactions to his work, and that you follow a sensible, gradual progressive training regime.

6–7 weeks	Horse can be regarded as half-fit for not-too-strenuous work – pleasure rides or drives, 2-hour hacks, half-a-day's gentle hunting, showing, dressage, short lessons and easy show-jumping
9–10 weeks	Horse is capable of competitive trail rides of up to 20 miles, a full day's hunting, lessons, active showing and hacking, more demanding dressage and show-jumping, eventing (not three-day), low-level polo, hunter trials and cross-country, and competitive trail rides
12–13 weeks	Horse can be regarded as fully fit for most purposes – competitive trail and endurance rides, racing, team chasing, strenuous hunting, active day rides, show-jumping, three-day eventing
13–16 weeks	Horse can be judged extremely fit for virtually any reasonable and sensible demands that may be made of him

job hopping

IF YOUR HORSE goes from job to job with the seasons, his fitness may well vary according to what he is doing but, for the general-purpose horse, there should be no great difference in the *level* of fitness aimed at, only in the type of schooling and gymnastic work required to get particular muscle groups fit and strong for the different disciplines. If, for instance, you compete mainly in indoor show-jumping in the winter and maybe hunt as well, and then do dressage and showing in the summer, the schooling you undertake will have to be adjusted with the seasons.

RESIDUAL FITNESS

Once a horse is about three-quarters fit, he can have around three weeks with no work at all without losing any significant fitness – provided he is turned out or kept moving in some other way. Therefore, your horse can have his breaks between seasons, between major competitions in your calendar or during your holidays or sickness without losing any appreciable ability to work.

Hacking on roads is essential for many owners in winter when ground conditions become too bad for riding offroad. It is important, though, to wear high-visibility clothing for safety – unlike these riders!

holidays for horse and owner

wish you were here

IF YOU'RE GOING AWAY and your horse will be left at home, you have to provide for his care in your absence. He may spend the time at grass so, from his viewpoint, the best seasons for a break are spring and autumn. Most horses do like to have a spell at grass with their friends, provided the weather conditions are comfortable.

If you keep your horse at home and there is going to be no reliable, knowledgeable member of the family or friend left to care for him, it would be safer for him to be sent to a reputable livery stable or riding centre. If he doesn't really need a rest and you have the money, this is also a good chance for him to receive some professional training.

If you keep your horse on a DIY livery yard, can you be absolutely certain that during your absence the other owners there will look after him properly, probably in exchange for your helping to look after theirs in similar circumstances? If not, your only alternative might be to pay a freelance groom to do him while you are away. This can also be arranged for horses kept at home, although you should consider the security risks as there will be no one on the premises for most of the time, unless the groom moves in.

Obviously, ensure that whoever is doing the honours while you are away has at least one telephone number (such as your mobile number) where you can be reached and be sure you have their mobile number, too. Your carer will also need the numbers of your veterinary practice and farrier, along with authorization to ring them – or others of their choice if yours is unavailable – should the need arise. Infected wounds, digestive problems, unusual lumps and loose shoes can all develop into emergencies if no one does anything about them. Don't forget to leave detailed feeding instructions (and ample supplies) and information about your horse's normal routine, behaviour and likes and dislikes.

horsey holidays
If your horse is going away with you, take a supply of his food, particularly hay or haylage, so as not to upset his digestion by any sudden changes. Most places will also insist on seeing his vaccination certificate and some will want to treat him for worms before he is allowed to graze their paddocks.

Your horse's packing to go on holiday will probably take just as long as your own! Don't set off without your horse, like a friend of mine did.

1 Never skimp the early stages of a fitness programme, otherwise your horse will not become properly fit and breakdowns and other injuries are more likely.

2 The first, slow phase of a fitness programme is needed as a basis for interval training, which is built on top after initial fitness is achieved.

3 A young horse who has never undergone a fitness programme will take longer to become fit than an experienced horse who has been fit before.

4 The fitter you want your horse ultimately, the longer must be his initial walking phase – allow up to a month, perhaps even six weeks if he is recovering from a leg injury.

5 You can save time and effort by starting off your fitness programme working your horse from the field for two weeks, unshod on yielding ground.

6 After six weeks, specialist schooling should be carried out according to your discipline.

7 Use opportunities while out hacking to school your horse and provide him with some variety.

8 Horses appreciate a holiday too from their normal work routine – a break of three weeks has no significant effect on the horse's fitness provided he is turned out a good deal.

3

Money
Matters

In our society there is very little you can do without money. Most people think they haven't got enough and very few admit to having too much. It is most noticeable that those who grumble that their wealth gives them problems never divest themselves of it in quantities sufficient to bring them down to the level of the rest of us! Money's advantages, it seems, definitely outweigh its disadvantages.

Horses come within the definition of 'expensive tastes'. They are expensive to buy yet not very profitable to sell (unless we are talking about high-class competition horses or bloodstock) and they are expensive to keep compared with other animal species. However, there is nothing wrong with cutting costs in horse keeping, and everything to be gained by sensible economies provided that the horses do not suffer. It might even make the difference between having one horse or two (maybe an outgrown pony to be turned to driving) or even keeping a horse at all.

Expenses can be cut drastically if you share a horse with someone else although disagreements may arise over use and management. This is especially likely if you do not own a share in the horse but merely help to pay the bills in exchange for riding and looking after him (which can be part of the fun, of course), so any sharing arrangement must be entered into carefully, preferably with a written agreement.

Similarly, if your horse is looked after free in exchange for your work or services with someone else's horses, or your horse's services as companion, you need to make sure that you retain your independence and do not end up being taken advantage of or paying far more in terms of time and effort than livery would cost you.

...nothing but the truth!

face up to it

Do not worry if, like most of us, you cannot afford a horsebox like this – such luxuries are not necessary. Careful budgeting will enable you to run your horse life as you wish, even when money is tight.

BEFORE YOU START a major cost-cutting operation, it is sensible to find out *exactly* how much your horse is costing you to keep over a full year. You may say 'I don't care how much he costs. He's my hobby and my pride and joy and I work hard to have him. I'll gladly pay out to keep him.' I know the feeling but that's no reason why you should pay out *unnecessarily*. Eking out your money is not mean – it is sensible. Indeed, it may mean the difference between having enough put aside to afford that veterinary emergency that your insurance won't cover or delaying calling the vet because the thought of the bill frightens you and then ending up with a seriously, and expensively, ill horse.

The more careful you are with what money you have, the more you can get for it and do with it.

So – sit down when you have time to concentrate and do the job properly. Write down absolutely everything from the past year that you can remember. Even if you have not kept your feed invoices, you will have a good idea how much your average bill is per week or month. You know how much you pay your farrier, your trainer, your livery stable. Also write down every little item of tack you bought, repairs, cleaning, your hairnets and his mints, riding club or hunt subscriptions, magazines, show entries and travelling expenses, and that new saddle. Ouch! If you don't include everything, you are lying to yourself.

When you have listed *everything*, add the figures up and divide them by 12 or 52 to arrive at the monthly or weekly amount your horse activities are really costing. If you haven't fallen over in a faint, improve matters by deducting any winnings.

To do things the accountant's way, take this total, deduct depreciation and find out how much interest you would have earned in a year in a basic savings account. If you keep your horse at home, ask yourself how much local taxes for your property would drop *without* the stabling, and so on, and add the difference to the calculations. To be even more cruel to yourself, you can also add the capital value of the horse and equipment to your imaginary savings account total, which should bump up your interest. All in all an entertaining evening's doodling.

your budget

NO BUSINESS CAN RUN without a budget. Most other operations, from households to private individuals also run to a budget, even though they may not realize it. You have to cut your coat according to your cloth, whatever your circumstances. A budget is just a money timetable (imagine the chaos of a school or public transport system with no timetable, the dentist, doctor or vet without an appointment system, and so on). It is a tell-at-a-glance way of seeing that your money is under control – or not.

Even if you have no business experience, you may have heard of something called a 'cash flow statement' or 'cash flow forecast'. This is just a crystal ball game in which you make estimates (glorified guesses) about how much money will be spent on a certain item in a certain month and how much money will come into the business in that same period. Then you make sure, by means of magic spells, prayers or hard work, that the money needed does come in at the time required. The amateur horse owner needs to allocate money regularly from salary or other income to make sure that his or her budget/money timetable is running to schedule.

how to do it First, take a large sheet of paper (say two A4 or foolscap sheets taped together down the middle). Rule a line across the top, one across the bottom for totals and add as many lines between as you have categories (livery, transport, and so on), plus a few more for forgotten items or new ones that will occur as you go along.

Next, rule the page vertically starting with a wide column on the left side, for your categories, and 26 more columns for figures – two for each month, plus two. Fill in your categories and then, above the horizontal line at the top of the page put 'January' over the first two figures columns, 'February' over the second two and so on to 'December'. Over the two final columns on the right put 'Totals'. (See p.41 for an example of a budget sheet.)

Now, multiply the figures you already have for the past year by the expected national inflation figure (your bank or accountant should give you an idea of this). Do not, though, then divide your estimate equally by 12 for a monthly figure as some will vary according to the season. Use your commonsense based on last year's actual events (and any receipts you have kept) and, keeping within your total, allocate a reasonable amount for each expense to each month – so for example, if your horse spends most of the winter stabled and most of summer turned away, you will need to allow more for concentrates and forage in the winter months and less in summer.

Put this expected cost (your budget or forecast figure) in the first (left-hand) column under each month. Do this for every item, every month. Then total each month and write in the figure in the relevant space on the 'totals' line that runs along the *bottom* of your sheet. Next, add up your categories across the columns and put each category total in the first of the two total columns running down the *right-hand side* of your sheet.

In the bottom right-hand corner you will have two blank total spaces. Add up all the totals along the bottom line and, in the left-hand space, pencil in the figure you get. Now add up all the totals in the column you have filled in down the right-hand side of the sheet. You should get the same total as the figure you have already pencilled in. If you do, this is said to 'balance'. Assuming it does, ink the figure in. You have completed your budget.

You still have as many blank columns as full ones. This is so that you can fill in your monthly expenditure for each category as you go along and put the appropriate monthly total actually spent (known as the 'actual' figure) on the right of your budget figure, so you can see how you are doing as the year progresses. It makes your sheet easier to read if you use one colour for the budget column and another for the actual column.

If your 'actuals' are regularly more than your 'budgets', you've got a problem. Either your sums were wrong in the first place, inflation is more than you expected, your costs have risen unexpectedly or your calculator batteries were running low when you did the budget, giving you some weird

figures. This is the benefit of having a carefully prepared budget – you can see what is happening and will be warned in plenty of time that you have to make economies in other areas or allocate more money from your income if you want to avoid overspending.

Should you be fortunate enough to be accumulating a surplus, instead of a deficit, you may go on a spending spree and buy a new saddle or a luxurious all-wool rug with your horse's name on it. On the other hand, if you were intending to buy a new saddle and/or rug or blanket but omitted to put the relevant cost into your budget, their subsequent purchase could play havoc with your money timetable and you will almost certainly show a deficit at the end of the year.

IN CONTROL

This is basically how a budget works and if you have never used one before you could be amazed what a tempering effect it has on your spending urges. It also gives you a self-satisfied glow when you see everything running according to plan, with your 'actuals' very near your 'budgets'. Should your end-of-year budget totals come within one per cent of your actual totals, apply to the Treasury for a job – your country needs you!

It is very wise to set up a 'contingency' or 'emergency' fund. As its name implies, this is a reserve fund to fall back on in unexpected, dire circumstances: you break your saddle tree, your trailer sustains four punctures, a gale whips the roof off your hay store and so on. This contingency fund can be large or small but should exist. You are sure to need it.

sample budget sheet

	JANUARY		FEBRUARY		MARCH		APRIL		MAY		JUNE		JULY		AUGUST		SEPTEMBER		OCTOBER		NOVEMBER		DECEMBER		TOTAL	
	Budget	Actual	Budget	Actual	Budget	Actual	Budget	Actual	Budget	Actual	Budget	Actual	Budget	Actual	Budget	Actual	Budget	Actual	Budget	Actual	Budget	Actual	Budget	Actual	Budget	Actual
Livery																										
Rent																										
Feed																										
Bedding																										
Farriery																										
Veterinary																										
Instruction																										
Horsebox/trailer maintenance																										
Petrol/diesel/oil																										
Tack (inc. repairs)																										
Horse clothing																										
Rider's clothing																										
Entry fees																										
Postage																										
Premises maintenance																										
Land care and maintenance																										
Hire of facilities (jumps, manège)																										
Subscriptions																										
Registration fees																										
Sundries																										
TOTAL																										

saving on livery

Try to avoid paying for facilities you can manage without. Some yards charge extra for using certain facilities, such as a horsewalker or even the indoor school.

IF, LIKE MOST PEOPLE, you have to keep your horse away from home, your biggest expense will be rent and livery charges, and in many places good livery stables are extremely hard to find. Some areas will be more expensive than others as the yard proprietor has to base charges on local costs such as taxes and business rates, the price of hay and so on. A yard just a very few miles further away can be significantly cheaper or dearer than one nearby. However, it is better to spend a bit extra to be sure of a good reliable place to keep your horse at and have peace of mind rather than to scrimp and be worrying about his welfare all the time.

Consider ways in which you might be able to pay a little less without compromising your horse's care. Your yard might charge more for stabling in a brick or concrete box than a wooden one because of the higher initial building costs, so if there is a wooden stable that has just as good ventilation, space and outlook, try to get that. Similarly, if your charge includes use of show-jumps and a cross-country course, but you and your horse never jump a stick, try to negotiate a reduction in your payment.

Try also to use a yard that will negotiate on price. There's no point in paying a full flat fee that includes services you never use. For instance, why pay for full grooming when you can do it yourself? And if your horse is not turned out to graze for some reason – perhaps because he is ill or the land is too wet – you should not be charged for use of the field during that period. You will be governed largely by the proprietor's pricing policy but there are ways of economising on livery charges so discuss these with the proprietor before moving your horse in and have them written into your contract (see p.19). If he or she won't negotiate, there's not much hope of a mutually beneficial working relationship in future.

If you are lucky enough have a choice of yards, it may be worth foregoing the indoor school or even outdoor arena, the automatic waterer in the box and the cross-country course you do not need and going for the cheaper, less impressive place that will still ensure your horse's wellbeing and happiness, especially if it is nearer your home and so quicker and cheaper to reach.

buying wise

IF YOU ARE RESPONSIBLE for buying your own equipment, feed and bedding, remember that good quality equipment works better and lasts longer, good quality feed is usually better for your horse and good quality bedding goes further and should not cause respiratory problems.

You may consider buying expensive things like tack, harness, rugs and blankets second-hand and this is fine, so long as you know what to look for (no cracked, stiff leather or worn, rotten stitching). Second-hand, good quality gear is far preferable to brand new, poor quality stuff. Used tack is often for sale at saddlers, but some sell it only for money and do not care about quality. If you go to a shop or store that is a member of a relevant specialist trade association, you should be assured of having access to expert advice as no reputable firm would stock shoddy gear, new or used.

bargains Other equipment, such as barrows, corn bins, brooms, shovels and so on, can often be bought at farm sales or auctions, but don't make the mistake of spending a lot of money on fuel getting there or paying transport costs getting your haul back home. Also, don't be tempted to buy something just because it is a bargain. If you don't need it, don't buy it. It's an easy way to waste money.

Buying good quality second-hand tack is preferable to being tempted by tack which may be shiny and new but can be lacking in quality.

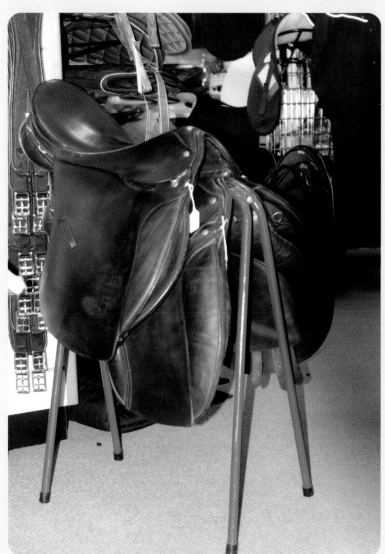

KITTY BUDGET

A kitty budget is an excellent scheme whereby all owners on a particular yard regularly pay an agreed amount per horse into a kitty. The money is then used to buy equipment such as mucking-out tools, headcollars, halters and ropes, a harrow for the land and so on. These items can be used by everyone. If there are, say, eight owners, it is unlikely that all of them will be mucking out at exactly the same time, so there is no point each person buying a full set of mucking-out tools. Two or three sets purchased from the kitty should be sufficient. (See also Getting Together, p.45.)

Look for ways of boosting the kitty budget, too. For example, you could get money from the sale of manure to plant nurseries, garden centres or private individuals. (If you're in an area where you have to pay to get rid of muck, fill empty feed sacks with it and offer it free at the gate of your premises, asking people to return the bags.)

how to avoid spending money

making do...

ONE OF THE MOST USEFUl items to have around the stable is a muck skep so that you can regularly remove droppings to avoid any more soiling of bedding than is absolutely necessary. Saddleries and tack shops sell these but there is no need to go out and buy one specially. Old dustbin lids and the lids of plastic mesh laundry bins make very servicable skeps; you can use the laundry bin itself for storing carrots and other roots. A laundry basket makes a good skep, too.

Many big name feeds are more expensive and not always better than others made regionally by lesser-known firms. An analysis of the contents should be on the bag or a label attached to it, so you can get a cheaper version that has all the nutritional value of the more well-known brand. If you don't fully understand analysis labels, check with your vet or an equine nutritionist to find out whether a feed is suitable and well balanced.

Feed supplements can be very expensive, so again check whether there is a cheaper one that is just as good. Also ask your vet whether, in fact, you need one at all; most good feeds contain a wide range of the most important vitamins and minerals and often supplements are not necessary, or may not really do what they claim to anyway.

...and spending sensibly

SOMETIMES IT'S very well worth spending money to save time and avoid really onerous work. For example, a *big* two- or four-wheeled muck barrow, though expensive, will repay its cost in saved effort and time in carting manure to the muck heap (see p.74).

absolutely minimal grooming kit	**1** Hoof pick (most important item) **2** Dandy brush **3** Plastic/rubber curry comb **4** Body brush **4** Metal curry comb **6** Two sponges – front end and back end (I use green and red respectively!)
absolutely minimal yard kit	**1** Fork (shavings or 4-tined for long straw) **2** Shovel **3** Hard-bristled stable/yard brush **4** Wheelbarrow (anything's better than none, but the large, 2-wheeled sort is best for one horse). They're expensive but you soon get sick of struggling with a muck sack
absolutely minimal tack	**1** Headcollar and rope (a minimum of 1.8m/6ft for tying up) **2** Saddle **3** Bridle **4** Boots (optional)
absolutely minimal rug wardrobe	None, if the animal is very hardy and not clipped. Otherwise: **1** Two turnout rugs **2** Two spring/autumn rugs plus under-rugs or **1** Two winter-weight rugs **2** Anti-midge sheet if the horse is susceptible to sweet itch/fly attacks

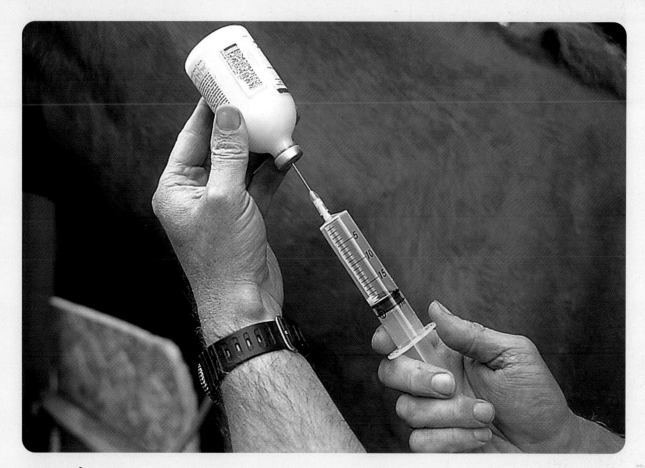

getting together

For routine veterinary work such as vaccinations, organize the vet to come for all the horses on the yard and save on travelling charges – check with your practice for details.

EVEN IF YOU DON'T MANAGE to organize a kitty budget (see box, p.43), you can get together with the other owners at your yard to take advantage of bulk-purchase prices for bedding, feedstuffs, professional contract transport to shows, veterinary supplies, such as wormers, and routine specialist services such as teeth checks, vaccinations and farriery. Vets and farriers are very busy people who would much rather see several horses on one visit than spend time tripping backwards and forwards (hence travelling charges). Veterinary practices often have group offers for routine work, and your farrier might charge less if he can shoe more than one horse during a visit. Freezemarking and micro-chipping are also cheaper if several animals are done together.

To make sure that savings on feed and bedding are fairly distributed, each owner works out how much their horse will need over a certain period. All amounts are then added together and a volunteer phones around for quotations for the bulk amount. When the invoice arrives, the total is divided up so that each owner pays their portion of the cost. This means that each owner buys only what they need but everyone enjoys the lower joint price.

natural savings

Cold horses eat more, so keep your horse warm *without* going over the top by muffling him up and leaving him in a stuffy stable. If you are doing light work, think seriously about not clipping him at all or only slightly. Only hard-working horses or ponies with thick greasy coats need a full or hunter clip. Those with any hot blood in them manage perfectly well, even in fast work, with a blanket or chaser clip. Chaser clips are used for steeplechasers and if they can be made fit with a partial clip, then it is good enough for any horse (see also p.129 and pp.132–133).

A lot of body heat is lost from the area between the buttocks, so don't pull your horse's tail but plait/braid it for special occasions so he has the benefit of protection at other times, especially if he is turned out a lot, as he will stand tail to the wind.

waging war on waste

Filling haynets is a chore but a good way to avoid waste. Arrange an old-fashioned clothes' horse in a triangle, hook the net inside it and you'll have both hands free to speed up the job.

WASTE IN FEEDING is expensive. Galvanized bins or hoppers for large yards not only keep your feed in good condition but are vermin-proof, which feed sacks are not. Plastic dustbins make a fair substitute. If a row of bins of the same height is neatly aligned, a pole can be passed through the handles on all the lids and fastened to the feed room wall, just as slip rails are fastened across a gateway, into a holder with a drop-down block of wood to prevent an escaped horse lifting it out.

Check for the 'use by' date on your feed sack, after this date the nutritional properties start to deteriorate and the feed might even go off, so your money will be wasted. Supplements are particularly sensitive to deterioration and must be stored according to directions – usually in cool, dark, dry conditions. Dried, chopped and often lightly syruped forages need storing indoors on a dry floor as moisture can enter through the ventilation holes.

If you like feeding straight grain (oats, barley, maize/corn) rather than prepared, branded concentrate mixes (sweet feeds) or cubes/pellets, don't buy more ready crushed, rolled or bruised grain than you can use in two weeks as it will then start to rot. Keep it dry and cool in storage.

Often little thought is given to storing hay. It needs to be kept dry. This is best done in a well-ventilated barn; if this is not possible raise it well off the ground (about 30cm/12in – or the height of a cat or terrier) and cover it with a tarpaulin or sheet of thick polythene that is tied down. Haylage and bagged, wilted forages can usually be stored outside, although they will be more vulnerable to rodents and birds pecking at the wrapping. Once opened, you should use a bale within four days, or seven at the most in cool weather, to maintain quality and safety in feeding.

Roots such as carrots and turnips keep best in airy, dark, cool places with the soil on. Wash them before feeding if they are not organic and only buy hard, crisp roots with no soggy patches.

ALTERNATIVE FORAGES

If hay and haylage prices shoot up in any particular year, consider using bagged forages, both long- and short-chopped, instead. Oat straw is a good fibre feed: it lacks protein, but this can be provided in a supplement – take expert advice on a suitable one.

feeding efficiently

Although a bit more time-consuming than feeding hay from the ground, feeding in a rack saves money as there is less spoilage. Racks like this ideally should also have a cover to protect the hay from being ruined by rain.

FEEDING LONG FIBRE in haynets or racks is a good way to prevent waste. Try to feed outdoor horses in a shelter to stop spoilage. Piling hay on the ground is extremely wasteful, but much quicker to do. Horses with quiet eating manners can be fed their fibre by putting it in plastic tubs or bins. This keeps it under some control and ensures that the horse has his head down to eat, which is good for digestion.

Quiet eaters can also have concentrates in a bucket or you can simply feed them on a clean piece of sacking on the floor. Horses who throw or blow their feed around, however, need a manger, either with bars across the corners or ends or with an in-turned lip to prevent the feed being scooped out. I don't recommend the 'waste rings' that can be fitted inside the top of the mangers; they really irritate most horses, as they need space for head movement when eating.

Although deep-litter bedding may be the cheapest method, it is not the healthiest. Research has shown that full mucking out is best and should be done while the horse is out of the box to prevent his inhaling spores and dust during the process. Shavings beds are impractical to muck out fully each day and most owners opt for semi-deep litter, lifting the bed fully at weekends when they have more time. Straw is usually cheaper than shavings but more work to manage (shredded straw is a better alternative). Urine is the main enemy of bedding – droppings, if removed frequently, are not so much of a problem. You can salvage half-dirty material by following the old practice of laying it out to dry somewhere – using time to save money. One sure-fire way of saving on bedding is to turn your horse out as much as possible.

best bedding

SAVING ON BEDDING is rarely simply a case of using the least pricey material you can get, particularly if your horse is sensitive and needs dust- or chemical-free bedding, which will be more expensive. You could start with the cheapest brand and try them all, keeping track of how much of each you need to use, the cost, how easy they are to muck out and how your horse gets on with them.

Rubber mats are increasingly popular, and there are as many views on their efficiency and hygiene as there are types and brands. Their main selling point is that you do not need bedding on top of them, but in my experience you definitely *do* need bedding, if not *quite* so much – about one quarter to one third less, in my experience. However, they are worth their investment in increased comfort and safety for the horse and the long-term saving on bedding (see also Flooring, p.49).

stabling economies

how you can save

Although horses can be reasonably content housed in conventional, individual stables, it is now thought that they should be able to touch and communicate with each other. Obviously, in any stable line-up, only compatible horses should be in neighbouring stables.

ECONOMIES ON STABLING can result in large savings. It is possible to construct loose boxes of basic design that are capable of accommodating horses healthily and well. The main needs are enough space, good ventilation, a view out (preferably on more than one side), shelter and dry, safe flooring. Strength to withstand a kicking, rubbing or pulling horse is essential. Any unsafe projections – wiring, pipes, and so on – must be removed or protected before the horse is installed. In addition, the construction materials (including the roofing, whether it is felt or tile) should insulate the interior, which must be cool in summer and not exactly cold in winter.

Brick and timber are both expensive, particularly if you have the refinements of double-skinned walls, double-insulated roof, overhang, ridge roof ventilators and so on. However, there are plenty of alternatives, ranging from various synthetic materials to concrete blocks. You might consider making the lower part of the wall brick or concrete block with wood higher up. Yorkshire boarding is an excellent choice for the upper walls, providing both shelter and excellent ventilation. It consists of planks running vertically with a space between each of about 6cm (2½in), which gives the horses a view out.

take into account
If you use buildings not originally intended as stables (see box, right) you need to be sure they are made safe. Ventilation is particularly important as stuffy atmospheres favour the development and spread of viruses and bacteria.

In addition, water pipes, such as those to automatic waterers, have to be protected from most horses, as does electrical wiring,

Being able to look out and about is important, and it is even better if horses have two viewpoints out of their stables.

CONVERSIONS

It is almost always cheaper to convert a suitable existing building than to build specially for the purpose, even taking into account the various improvements that might be required. The most common conversions are farm buildings. A problem with these is that they often have low ceilings, which are dangerous and make for poor ventilation, as do the lack of windows, louvres or other decent air-flow devices. They are, in short, usually dark and stuffy, so expenditure on improving these faults is necessary. Large barns, old shippons, byres or milking parlours are good candidates for economical conversion and usually have lofty ceilings. Even so, more ventilation may need to be installed.

the most usual way being to build conduits or at least strong metal guards around them. The floors may be uneven or of slippery concrete or broken bricks and will need attention.

Horses feel happier with a good view so try to allow each one the means to put his head outside or at least look at his surroundings. They also like to be able to see and touch each other. Make your dividing walls around 1.5m (5ft) high, so they can easily talk with no risk of climbing or jumping over. If they know each other well, the walls can be lower and they can do mutual grooming. The lower the walls, the less material you have to buy. Always avoid stabling enemies next to each other – this is very bad management.

second-hand Savings can be made by using second-hand materials. Look around salvage yards and watch your local paper for advertisements of farm sales where buildings are being dismantled. You should save enough to make the transport worthwhile. Just remember that your resulting reconstruction needs to be very strong. When tied up a horse can exert a pull of two and a half times his own weight. A persistently kicking horse can easily crack a strong brick or block wall. Lining the walls

with padded vinyl, rubber or something similar is a big help. The best answer is to stop the horse kicking, but sometimes it is impossible to find any reason for it; there are occasions when you have to bring your horse in, and if you've got a kicker, you have to protect your investment: both building and horse.

flooring When making your stables, if you have a choice, try to lay floorings that let urine drain through – such as loose-laid bricks on a gravel base or loose-weave asphalt laid over gravel and not tamped down; both these are excellent but rarely seen.

A simple earth floor, as often used in hot climates, with bedding on top works well in dry areas. The siting of the stables must be very carefully considered as any water seepage into them can turn the floor into a quagmire. Local authorities might object on grounds of poor hygiene. I like earth floors as they are warm in winter and cool in summer and I find that there is no residual wet from urine, the bedding stays quite dry and there is no smell. You use less bedding than on other floors, especially concrete, which is a bad flooring (cold, very hard and holds urine). A bonus is that horses find earth floors with bedding comfortable to lie on.

stabling economies

yarding or corralling

YARDING AND CORRALLING are very economical ways of accommodating horses so long as adequate shelter is also provided, which is not usually the case with corrals. Most places don't make the best use of their facilities and land: nearly every stables has a disused or untidy building that could easily be converted to a shed with an open pen in front for horses or ponies (see also p.11).

The shed could be bedded down on deep litter with the droppings removed twice daily – being open-fronted, it will be well ventilated – which is much less trouble than mucking out a stable. If the pen hasn't got an earth surface, it should be topped with sand, woodchips or something similar. A shed for two horses should be at least 5m (16ft) by 3.5m (12ft) and will be much cheaper to construct than two individual stables.

Apart from your savings in time, effort and money, yarding and corralling are very popular with horses, particularly if several are in together. They learn herd manners and, as a result, take to human discipline much more readily. Hay/haylage can be fed in large head-height racks running round the building and concentrates in individual buckets with someone staying to prevent thieving and bullying.

CHORES – TIME AND MONEY

The only way to save money on paid labour is not to employ it. This means that you do the work yourself, get someone to do it for you or take turns with other owners in a communal yard to help each other out (see Group Action, pp.56–63).

There are mechanical ways of saving routine work, including horsewalkers, electric groomers, heat lamps, and simple options such as riding one horse and leading one or two others – if you have safe facilities and sensible, obedient horses. Turning out horses also exercises them without you having to take the time.

Mucking out is one of the most time-consuming chores. Although deep litter is not healthy in the long run, if you are desperately busy for a day or two, there is nothing wrong with just picking up droppings and putting down new bedding until you have more time, but this does make a bigger job for you later.

farriery

Farriery is a very significant outlay for most owners but you should never economize on it to the detriment of your horse's feet and his comfort.

SHOEING IS EXPENSIVE. You'll probably spend much more on your farrier than your vet. Apart from hoof growth having to be pared back, a horse doing two hours' work a day, much of it on roads, will wear out a set of shoes in six weeks or less. Using heavier shoes is not the answer as it causes the feet to go down with more force, creating more wear on the shoe and more concussion on the foot and leg. One way of reducing wear is to ride on verges or tracks where possible. Another is to ask your farrier if he will weld a hardener such as boron (or anything that wears rough, not smooth, to help prevent slipping) into areas of the shoe that are subject to most wear.

Many animals are shod unnecessarily. If you work mainly on soft surfaces or, for limited distances, hard, smooth roads, and your horse's foot conformation and horn quality are good, he might be able to go barefoot and will develop harder horn in the long-term. Discuss this with your farrier.

travelling

Trailers are much more economical to buy and run than horseboxes, but ensure you get a strong, stable and reliable make that is big enough for your horses, and keep it very well maintained.

IF YOU DO a lot of travelling, it is cheaper and more convenient to have your own horsebox or trailer, even if you mothball it out of season to save road tax. Although more expensive to run and maintain, horseboxes score every time over the less safe and less comfortable but certainly cheaper trailers. With trailers you have no road tax (depending on which country you live in) but there is an added cost on your car insurance. Your car's transmission will suffer more wear and you might need a larger more powerful one, possibly an off-roader, particularly if you are going to carry two or more horses.

Clubbing together with friends for contract transport is fairly economical. Do not, in pursuit of excessive economy, be tempted to put up with a vehicle that is unroadworthy or uncomfortable and unsafe for the animals travelling in it.

If you get a lift from a friend be sure there is no question of it being a 'hire and reward' arrangement (ie make sure that you do not pay for the service, other than money for fuel) as, if it is, you could find that your friend's insurance cover is negated. Some insurance policies only cover the holder for their own animals, too. Similarly, check your own policy to find out if it covers you to carry other people's horses, even for free.

insurance

getting covered

HORSE INSURANCE CAN BE a nightmare, and I feel can often be a major moral fraud. Problems often occur when the company vet disagrees with your vet over significant problems, including euthanasia and loss of use, the premium for the latter usually being uneconomical, at least in Britain. Many owners feel that it is only worth having third party insurance (which is free for certain British Horse Society members in the UK) and veterinary fees insurance. A difficulty with the latter is that if a claim is made for a particular ailment one year, the next year the premium is raised or that problem has been excluded from cover. It is never worth delaying calling the vet because of this. Some vets are willing to challenge insurance companies on behalf of their clients, often tenaciously and successfully.

If you see brochures for particular insurance companies at your practice, you should be able to rely on them, and other owners will have opinions, too. Some veterinary practices will not treat horses whose insurance is with certain companies known not to pay out. On the plus side, premiums may be reduced if your horses are on dust-free bedding and feed, never travel, do low-risk jobs or are security marked. In addition, some aspects may be included in your household policy, such as tack if the tack room is part of the house. If not you may need to buy separate insurance and install special security devices, or consider taking your tack home.

In general, *do* be quick to jump on unfairness or unethical behaviour and *don't* be intimidated by your insurance company. Do not accept judgements on health matters given by non-veterinary personnel at the company. Do not be fobbed off with irrelevant excuses such as 'it's standard practice' – that doesn't make it right or acceptable. Use the insurance ombudsman if faced with unethical or unreasonable treatment. Get clear written explanations about ambiguous policy clauses and don't use a company with a poor reputation or with which you are dissatisfied.

Insurance for loss of use and euthanasia can be extremely expensive. However, depending on what you use your horse for, it may be well worth being covered. Talk to other owners and get quotes from various companies before making a decision.

✓ Feed concentrates in tip-proof containers or hold the bucket of a messy feeder to prevent waste.

✓ Make sure that hay cannot be trampled in the mud or blown away.

✓ Feed short-chopped forages in large, deep mangers or tubs on the floor, maybe tied to the wall, so that they can be given ad lib as an alternative or additional source of fibre to hay or haylage. These feeds take longer to chew than long forage and should reduce the intake of the latter.

✓ Effective worm control is one of the two best methods of saving money on feed, even taking into account the cost of drugs. You save on veterinary bills, too, as parasite-infested horses suffer poorer health and can die because of the effects of worms.

✓ Proper dental care is the other main way of saving on feed. Teeth should be checked every quarter for young and old animals and every six to 12 months for others.

✓ Keeping a horse warm with comfortable clothing is an excellent way of saving feed and preserving health. Overdoing rugs, however, has the reverse effect, distressing the horse and triggering skin problems.

✓ Never skimp on a horse's fibre. Expensive concentrates should be regarded as a back-up or top-up to fibre of the right nutrient grade and energy level for your horse.

✓ Keep feed in damp- and vermin-proof containers to avoid waste from contamination. Use an old fridge for summer storage of perishable feeds like supplements, soaked sugar beet and the like.

✓ Check with a nutritionist before buying expensive equine feeding oils. Corn, sunflower and soya oils may be just as good and are cheaper at your supermarket.

✓ Make feed measures by cutting the bottom off a lemonade bottle and sticking on a label stating how much, by weight, of each feed it holds.

✓ Weigh out feeds accurately. Feeding too much is expensive and wasteful and can adversely affect your horse's health and behaviour.

✓ Don't buy more perishable feed than you can use within a safe period (stated on the bag of branded feeds) as it will deteriorate and be wasted.

✓ Don't store hay where it is exposed to the rain and snow as this leaches out nutrients and makes it inedible, creating waste.

✓ Soak hay for only about five minutes otherwise nutrients seep out. A thorough wetting may be just as good.

✓ Well-cared-for grass of a suitable type for your horse or pony is far cheaper than bought-in feeds and may be just as good.

✓ It's cheaper to keep your horse at a commune-type stable, where you take it in turns to do each other's chores, than to pay livery fees; it also cuts down your number of trips to the yard.

✓ Buy in bulk when you can, maybe with friends, as it should be cheaper than buying in smaller quantities. If it isn't, ask for a quantity discount.

✓ Save twine from hay and straw bales, also the thread from the tops of feed sacks, if you can get it to unravel as it should. These are useful for many things from making haynets and doing running emergency repairs to blankets and rugs and fencing to producing fillet strings, halters and headcollars and more.

✓ Make your own haynets/bags out of binder/baler twine.

✓ Use plaited/braided twine to make double-length leadropes that loop through the jaw ring on your headcollar for leading. You don't need clips and they are safer because if the horse breaks free and treads on the rope it will pull through, rather than bringing him down.

✓ A thick bed is more economical and effective than a thin one: you throw out less material in the end.

✓ Identity-coding your horse is cheaper and less painful than replacing him.

✓ Keep vaccinations current so you don't have the expense of re-doing the whole programme.

✓ Arrange farriery and veterinary visits on the same day as other owners at your stables to reduce visit charges.

✓ Run a horsey car boot/yard sale. As well as getting cash for your unwanted bits and pieces, you could buy some bargain items (if genuinely needed!) from others.

✓ Some tack shops sell unwanted equipment on commission. As you will probably buy supplies when you collect your cash, this is good for them and you.

✓ Buy the best quality you can afford of everything as it will last much longer, but never pay just for a 'name' – often their quality and design are no better than cheaper makes.

✓ Don't be swayed by advertising hype. Before you buy *anything* be sure that it will benefit you or your horse.

✓ For short periods in the field, diluted home antiseptics or a vinegar and cold tea mixture make good insect repellents. Garlic in the feed has a similar effect, as does a wash made with lavender essential oil.

✓ Disposable nappies/diapers are good for retaining heat on legs or feet when poulticing or applying hot or cold packs.

✓ Ask your farrier if he thinks that welding hardening materials into the most worn parts of your horse's shoes, for extra wear, would be a sensible idea.

✓ Learn to do simple tack and clothing repairs yourself.

✓ It's cheaper to ask a saddler to alter items of tack than to buy new ones. For example, a running martingale can be made into a standing one, a cavesson noseband can be adapted to become a flash, and a bridle can be made bigger or smaller.

✓ You can make a good bitless bridle out of a *strong* drop noseband and a pair of reins.

✓ Rather than buying new, get good quality, guaranteed, used tack from a reputable saddler and have it altered to fit your horse, if necessary.

✓ 'It's not what you can do *with*, it's what you can do *without*' (A friend).

✓ Use second-hand wood for fence repairs and jumps.

✓ House train your horse. Train him to associate, say, a particular, low whistle with staling, then you can get him to urinate on command outside the stable and on rides. Get him used to staling into a bucket with a little bedding in the bottom (to avoid the noise and splash, which horses hate). Most horses want to stale after work and on a new bed, so be ready with the bucket.

✓ Keep your insurance premiums up-to-date so you don't lose out if you need to claim.

4

Group Action

There is a great deal to be said for independence, but just as much for being part of a group, even a small one, of like-minded people who work together to help each other out, either just during emergencies or to make life easier for themselves and each other. A livery 'commune' can be an ideal way to keep a horse. The premises can be rented privately or you can all keep your horses at a DIY livery stable or at the home of one of the owners. In the latter case, the owner of the premises will probably not want to charge his or her co-owners rent, as this would make it a formal business.

The idea is that you all basically look after your own horses but help each other out when circumstances require it, such as someone having transport problems or being sick or on holiday – or simply exhausted with other things. You can also arrange a semi-formal rota for set days for particular people to be on duty. Individual owners are responsible for all their own costs of feed, bedding, shoeing, veterinary expenses and so on, and, if applicable, rent for stabling and grazing, but not for labour. In turn, it is understood that everyone has to do their fair share within a mutually acceptable agreement.

Such arrangements can work extremely well, provided you all get on together. In particular, you won't want anyone involved whose ideas of horse care differ drastically from your own, who you do not like or trust, who is unreliable or simply to whom you can't talk. You must all agree on exactly how the horses are going to be cared for, and this can cause concern and dissatisfaction if people's principles differ significantly. Everyone must be clear about the amount of work and time involved, maintenance and repair costs, worming, vaccinations, grazing and play areas and times, not to mention companions, and general give and take. If the scheme gets going and someone is clearly not pulling their weight, it must be agreed that they get one warning and if they don't improve, they're out.

do-it-yourself livery

a co-op

COMMUNES CAN WORK WELL within a commercial DIY livery yard – the most common form of livery as it is the cheapest. Like any other system, it has advantages and disadvantages. The best DIY places have a responsible manager who oversees owners and horses without interfering unless necessary. Owners do their horses according to their own principles, but the manager should deal with any cases of neglect or mistreatment. In an ideal situation, the person concerned will have matters explained to them so that they know better in future; those who refuse to improve will, it is hoped, be required to leave, perhaps with a simultaneous report to an animal welfare organization, too.

Major problems can arise where the premises have no living accommodation and so there nobody is around overnight or even during the day. This leaves horses wide open to theft and abuse and is very risky. Security should be really tight (see also pp.88–93). In addition, where there is no manager or no formal supervision of any kind, problems tend to be common, with irresponsible or uncaring horse owners

GOOD NEIGHBOURS

On DIY yards, even if your security arrangements are good, keeping friendly with your neighbours can be really helpful. Ask them to tell you if they see anything suspicious, and return the favour. A card, a plant and a bottle of wine or box of chocolates at Christmas would not go amiss!

Running a yard as a co-op can be a cheap form of livery and work well if all the owners pull their weight and have similar horse management beliefs.

neglecting or abusing their animals. Unlike a managed yard where the reputation of the establishment should matter to the proprietor, unsupervized yards have no one who cares about this sort of thing. The other owners have no one to whom to report problems and may have to look after their own horses in an unpleasant, slapdash atmosphere with which they will not be happy. However, the bottom line is that each horse's welfare is the responsibility in law of its owner, not the yard proprietor or manager or other commune members although, should a case go to court, the proprietor or manager could be regarded as accessories.

many hands

THERE IS EVERYTHING to be gained by all the owners in a DIY livery yard, particularly one with no manager or proprietor supervizing, getting together and working out ways in which they can all help each other. Co-operation arrangements are generally more successful where there are

A GROWN UP WAY TO KEEP HORSES

Any horse needs attending to at least twice in 24 hours. For one person, this involves two trips, two lots of fuel or fares, two lots of commuting time and two lots of chores to perform, but even if only two friends or associates get together and agree that one does the horses in the morning and the other at night, on specified days of the week, think how much easier it could be.

only a few owners. The bigger the yard, the more likely it is that there will be at least a few people who prefer to keep themselves to themselves and simply don't want to get involved in other people's responsibilities, and that's fair enough.

let's get together To start up a livery commune, why not call an informal meeting either in the stables or at someone's home and put forward your ideas of how you could all help each other? If your yard does have a manager, he or she could certainly be invited as the linchpin of the operation, maybe not actually being roped in with the work, except in genuine emergency or by pre-arrangement, but seeing that messages reach the right people and that each horse is properly cared for.

To make any communal arrangement work you all have to be reasonable people – individuals, obviously, with your own ideas and standards of knowledge, but able to work together with two main aims:

To ensure that all the horses and ponies on the yard are properly looked after

To save each other time and money by helping each other reliably

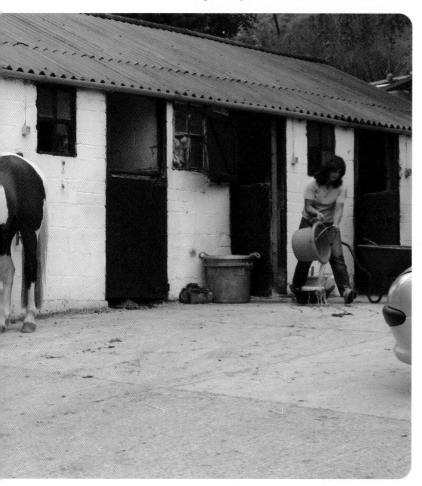

how the rota system works

THIS IS A TYPICAL communal yard, purely imaginary but based on existing ones. It comprises the following people with their differing time availability and hours of work:

1 A young secretary whose job is mainly nine-to-five Monday to Friday but who occasionally works flexitime
2 A hospital doctor who works long erratic hours and who is sometimes at the yard on weekdays
3 A production worker who does a regular shift rota (three 5am to 1pm shifts, three 1pm to 9pm shifts and three 9pm to 5am shifts followed by three days off)
4 A shop assistant who works mainly 9am to 5.30pm but all day most Saturdays with two varying half-days off during the week
5 A vicar who is never at the yard on Sundays but often attends during the day on Saturdays and weekdays
6 Two teenagers who are at a nearby school and see to their ponies morning and late afternoon Monday to Friday and, of course, nearly all weekend, plus school holidays
7 A freelance instructress who cares for her horse when she is not teaching
8 A proprietor who takes messages and generally oversees operations to make sure every animal is properly looked after but doesn't want to become too involved

A rota has been drawn up through mutual discussion and agreement. It may change frequently according to each owner's availability, and is written on a board in the tack room. Those with irregular working hours write on it when they will be available. In every case, when one owner's allotted jobs cannot be done because of his or her unavoidable absence, someone else takes over.

The secretary's salary is moderate so instead of paying rent to the proprietor she helps her with correspondence and office work on a regular basis. She can arrive at her job at 10am on certain days, provided that she makes up the time at some point by staying until 6pm. She usually does this as the two teenagers come to the yard straight from school and can be there to see to her horse at 4.30pm, in exchange for her having fed theirs and turned them out in the morning.

The shop assistant and the instructress are both present early each day and do the horses whose owners are not coming that morning, feeding and turning out according to the owners' instructions, as noted in a 'master diary' in the tack room (see pp.82–85).

On her afternoons off, the shop assistant often exercises someone else's horse as well as her own in exchange for them exercising hers on Saturdays, when she cannot normally be present. The instructress is sometimes away for a couple of days taking courses and clinics but repays the others for looking after her horse during these times by giving them free lessons and help with schooling problems.

Most owners are present over the weekend so the vicar's horse is cared for on Sunday. In exchange, he fits in jobs as he can during the week, looking on the board and in the diary to see what needs doing. This also applies to the shift worker.

The proprietor keeps the board and master diary up-to-date by writing in owners' phone messages and on the rare occasions when no one at all can be present at a certain time she will feed, skip out, water and bring horses in and out from the field. If her duties become significantly time-consuming, the owners pay for them separately from their rent out of the kitty budget (see p.43).

I once kept a horse in a DIY yard with no manager. It was owned by an elderly, but fairly active lady who would not enter a stable but would always help by throwing in hay and filling buckets over doors with a hosepipe. Our kitty budget regularly paid for the services of a freelance groom and the system worked very well, particularly as

Rotas for turning out and bringing in each other's horses can save you having to make trips to the yard at inconvenient times and help to make everyone's lives that much easier.

the owner lived on the premises and we had two shift workers among us who could usually be present when the rest of us could not.

common sense plus As you can see, a group of people can work together to ensure that while they still have time to enjoy their own horses, all the animals in the yard are looked after at least adequately by means of common sense, fair play and organization. They all know each other's animals and their foibles well and take an interest in them, so they gain a wider experience of horses and horsemastership than would be the case if they restricted their activities to just their own horse.

you're on your own

the buck stops here

IF YOU KEEP YOUR HORSE at home and do not want, or haven't room for, other people's horses, you may be able to rope in at least one member of the family to help while you are at work or away, or you could consider paying for the occasional services of a freelance groom. Local agencies should have a pool of temporary and occasional help on which you can draw, so keep the phone numbers of at least two handy, as well as a list of individual freelancers. Agencies and freelancers usually advertise in regional horse magazines. Other than this you will simply have to manage by means of super-organized efficiency and willpower. If your whole family is going on holiday together, send the horses away to livery rather than keeping them at home in the hands of a temporary groom who only comes in morning and evening. You might get away with leaving them at home alone if you have a very close neighbour who will help, but personally I would not want to leave a horse of mine unsupervized for any long periods of time.

Knowing and using exact measures for horse feed is crucial to maintain your horse's health especially when he is being fed by someone else.

FEED IT RIGHT

Probably the single aspect of horse management most likely to cause problems when horses are being looked after by someone other than their owner is feeding. It is essential, where others are involved, to leave clear and precise details of what your horse should have for each feed, either in a book, on a chart on the wall or on a communal board used for everyone on the place. Put exact details in weight rather than simply saying 'a scoop of this' and 'a spoon of that', for reasons of both general health and economy.

Horses have very delicate digestive systems and will not tolerate too many irregularities in feeding – write it all down so that there cannot be any misunderstandings.

1 The first essential is a group of responsible, mature and reasonable people who each have enough common sense and knowledge to look after other people's horses and who recognize an emergency when they see one.

2 Make sure everyone in the scheme has third party insurance.

3 A place with a manager or helpful, knowledgeable proprietor is a big plus.

4 It is crucial to be able to rely on and trust the other people involved in your horse's care, otherwise your life will be a constant nightmare of worrying and wondering – and so will your horse's.

5 Work out a mutually agreed rota and maintain a master diary (see pp.82–85) for routines, messages and instructions. On arrival at the stables, first look quickly round all the horses, out or in, then refer to the diary to keep up-to-date with the current situation.

6 Have everyone's contact numbers – owners, veterinary practices and farrier – easily to hand.

7 Run a kitty budget (see p.43) to which everyone contributes regularly and into which money from the sale of muck can also go.

8 Keep the phone numbers of agencies and freelance grooms for times when there just aren't enough hands to do the jobs.

9 Give those who don't pull their weight or make too many mistakes one warning; if they don't improve, they're out of the scheme. Be ruthless for the sake of your horses.

10 Don't move the goalposts without mutual agreement. Be very clear among yourselves about work, time and costs so everyone knows what is expected.

5

Make Time

We all have the same amount of time – 24 hours in each day-night cycle – yet how often do working horse owners complain, 'I haven't got time to do that'? Of course, what we really mean is that there is too much else to do. If this applies to you (and it applies to most people who go out to work and also own a horse), try thinking seriously not only about how much you commit yourself to – in your horse life and the rest of it – but also about how you decide what is most important.

If any of the following apply to you, the chances are that you are genuinely doing too much, or not doing what you do efficiently, or not getting your priorities right.

You constantly feel pressured

You find it hard to concentrate on what you are doing NOW and are always thinking about what you have to do next, tomorrow, next week or next month

You become bad tempered easily, even with those you love

You frequently feel tired, not healthily physically tired but draggingly weary

You do not seem to get much real enjoyment out of life, not even from your horse, that you are supposed to be keeping for fun

set priorities

getting time on your side

Opposite: Involving the whole family in each other's interests, whether horses or other things, is healthy for your relationships and can be fun.

SO LIFE IS getting you down, but there's plenty you can do about it. Time management has long been big in the business world and all the often very expensive courses run on this topic are based on one fundamental principle:

To manage your time effectively you have to get your priorities right

You need to learn to evaluate your tasks accurately so that you are sure which are the most important – these are not necessarily those that are the most *urgent* because you'll have to do them anyway. Write down your daily tasks in the order in which they need to be done – as if you had to give someone else the work. Writing them down will crystallize everything wonderfully for you. The list will act as an ever-present personal assistant and you will get a super feeling of smugness and self-satisfaction when you look at it at the end of the day, all crossed off because everything has been done. You can usefully extend listing your priorities to other areas of your life as well as your horse – home/family/pets, work/business/studies, hobbies/social life/friends – and in this way you'll get a clear picture of the whole of your life's activities so you can see if any one aspect is taking a disproportionate precedence over the others.

putting your horse first

THE KEY TO GETTING your horse-task priorities right is straightforward. *You simply put first those jobs that DIRECTLY affect your horse.* Another list! Write down every single daily job – large or small – that you have to do (or think you have to do) for or because of your horse. Now divide the main list into two separate lists – A jobs and B jobs. The A jobs are those that directly affect your horse and the B jobs are those that are connected with him but do not directly affect his wellbeing.

CONSIDER THIS

Wondering how on earth you are going to get everything done is just about the worst way to spend your time. During the time you are wondering, you are actually doing precisely nothing which is not just a complete WASTE of time; it's an aggravating, depressing way of doing nothing too, when you could be chilling out with a self-satisfied 'I deserve this' feeling because you've accomplished your most important tasks.

For example, to help you prioritize, put yourself in your horse's position and imagine what he would care about:

- He would care about getting his food
- He would like to have clean water to drink
- He would enjoy getting out of his box and stretching his legs
- He would love some effective shelter in his field where he could get away from extremes of weather
- He would care about having somewhere away from his own excreta to stand and lie
- He would like to have friends to socialize with (not just look at over his door)
- He would appreciate his rugs being comfortable

On the other hand, he couldn't care less about straw blowing about the yard, about paintwork peeling, about the untidy tack room or the sprawling muck heap.

Overleaf are lists of possible A and B jobs to provide you with the tools to set accurate priorities, ensure your horse is superbly cared for and give you more time to relax.

set priorities

A jobs

A-list jobs should take priority during your horse time – all are very important because they directly affect the horse

- Feeding and watering
- Mucking or skipping out – stable and/or field
- Adjusting, changing or washing rugs
- Cleaning feed and water containers
- Maintaining the stable (so that it is safe and effective)

- Maintaining the field shelter (so that it is safe and effective)
- Maintaining fencing and gates (so that the horse can be turned out)
- Exercising – ridden, from the ground or at liberty with his friends
- Picking out feet, sponging sensitive bits – eyes, nose, lips, under the tail, sheath or udder
- Brushing off mud and dried sweat from the head, saddle and girth areas, or whole body if the horse wears rugs or blankets
- Washing the bit, and cleaning parts of tack that touch the horse
- Ordering and collecting feed and bedding

Two vital A jobs – picking up droppings for parasite control and mending fences so that your horse can have his all-important turn out.

B jobs

B-list jobs, although important, do not directly affect the horse and so should not take priority over A jobs when you are really pushed for time

Don't worry about your muck heap. Just keep it bearably tidy. It will rot down on its own and you have got better things to do.

- Full grooming or strapping (nearly an A job)
- Sweeping the yard
- Stacking feed, hay or bedding
- Full tack cleaning
- Full grooming kit cleaning
- Painting woodwork
- Tidying the tack room
- Cleaning tools (other than grooming kit)
- Tending the muck heap (in fact, this is a D job!)

Don't be horror struck at my B list. If you have a job to do, a business to run and/or a young family or elderly relatives to look after, your time really is very limited and it is quite possible for one horse to take up a whole working day if you let him. Work really does expand to fill the time available. Turn things around and make the chores diminish so that you can spend more of your valuable time doing the things you really want to do, such as riding your horse or just being with him, rather than sweeping the yard, cleaning your tack meticulously, rooting out drawers or cleaning the tack room windows.

I have a particular aversion to spending my time looking after a muck heap. I cringe every time I hear someone say, 'A tidy muck heap is a sign of a tidy mind'. In the case of a working horse owner (whether that work brings in money or not), a tidy muck heap is a sign of someone who hasn't got their priorities right. The state of your horse and your family and your friends is far more important than the state of your muck heap.

If all your A jobs are done and your horse is either contentedly munching away in his box, having had pleasant, slightly taxing exercise or training, or in the field grazing and enjoying the company of his friends, then it is time to get stuck into those B jobs – you've nothing more important to do.

- A pair of extra large rubber gloves over the top of ordinary gloves makes handling wet/soaked hay much easier.

- Put an old tennis ball in your water trough to stop it freezing over. An old but clean plastic feed sack filled loosely with straw and sealed works equally well when laid over the trough after all the horses have come in for the night.

- Use an old cool box for soaking sugar beet – it won't freeze in very cold weather.

- Save water by steaming your hay instead of soaking it – a large plastic dustbin is ideal. Put your hay net in the bin, pour over a kettle full of boiling water, put the lid on and leave for an hour.

- Rub udder cream on chapped hands.

- Buy some bucket covers so you can fill your water buckets in the morning, ready for the evening and protect them from dust and birds.

- Make up evening feeds in the morning to save a few minutes later on in the day – or make up several at the weekend (put them in plastic bags and out of the reach of vermin). Don't damp them otherwise they'll go sour and soggy.

- Use a headlamp, like cavers and potholers wear, during the dark winter evenings – they leave both hands free.

- Just like your horse, make sure you have two waterproof jackets so one can dry while the other is being worn.

- Pocket handwarmers, available from camping stores, allow you to warm your hands while you have a spare moment.

- Make up a week's worth of hay nets at the weekend when you have more time (and daylight).

- A little baby oil in your horse's mane and tail keeps the mud at bay.

- Grease your horse's heels with baby oil/vegetable oil or udder cream to stave off mud fever.

- Use an old broom handle or piece of drainpipe to rig up a line in a warm place to hang wet rugs to dry overnight.

- Tie a hoof pick to your skip bucket and pick out your horse's feet straight into the bucket – you won't lose your pick and there will be less mess on the yard to sweep up later.

- Old washing baskets are great for mucking out shavings beds – the dung and heavier wet shavings are collected while dry shavings fall back out through the holes.

- Invest in a waterproof cover for your leather saddle – it will save you time caring for wet leather.

- A waterproof exercise sheet will help keep your horse dry, thus saving you time drying him off after a ride.

- Rubbing a little leather oil or dressing into your leather bridle and saddle will make rain run straight off it rather than soak in. Alternatively, wipe your tack clean with a damp cloth then use leather oil before soaping.

- If your horse has muddy legs, hose them off and put on clean, dry stable bandages to dry them and help prevent mud fever.

- Remember that the water you spill in the yard this evening might be a sheet of ice tomorrow morning. Sweep up water spills straight away and put salt or sand on top.

- Always keep a dry pair of gloves handy, and buy yourself a really warm hat to wear around the yard – it will be worth every penny.

- Keep a spare set of clothing in your locker at the yard, or in your car. When you get soaked riding you can change into dry clothes, rather than driving home wet.

- Consider keeping a set of riding clothes at the yard, so you can go for an inpromptu ride after work one evening if the mood takes you.

- Get together with other owners to buy large sacks of carrots – it'll be much cheaper and between you all you'll use them before they go off.

- Cut down on brushing your horse's tail. Use plenty of mane and tail dressing to keep it clean and rub dried mud off between your hands.

- Have a set day/evening when you clean tack and wash numnahs and so on – that way they get done regularly, not just when you remember.

- Attach baler twine to a dishwashing brush and tie it to the tap so it's always there when needed.

- When opening bales, cut the twine near the knot and hang the lengths up somewhere convenient for all those mending jobs – gates, haynets, leadropes and so on

- Hang up peeled and cut onions in the stables to ward off respiratory diseases. Change on a weekly basis.

fine tuning

work smartly, not hard

A definite A-list job! You can gain more exercising time by working a little bit quicker and getting through your chores in less time.

MAKE SURE YOU DON'T waste valuable horse time, or daylight hours in winter, by, for example sweeping the yard when your horse needs exercising. Get him out first, feed him, make him comfortable and sweep the yard (if you must) by electric light.

Working a little quicker is a definite asset. If it normally takes you half an hour to groom your horse and half an hour to muck out his box, allow 25 minutes for each task and you will save ten minutes, which you can use to clean feed and water containers or stay out ten minutes longer at exercise or run over the underside of your bridle, a job that might otherwise not get done. Imagine that you have only half an hour before you have to leave to pick up your daughter from dancing class. There are two jobs left to do: grooming and yard sweeping. Which one wins? Grooming, of course.

Now imagine that the horse needs both grooming and mucking out, both half-hour A-list jobs, and you only have half an hour. Why not dandy him over and sponge his sensitive bits, pick out his feet then remove the droppings and dirtiest bedding, filling in with some clean stuff? That way, you have ensured your horse's immediate comfort and will be in time to collect your daughter.

make a timetable

TRY SETTING OUT a timetable showing what you should be doing and when. This might sound regimented but in practice it can give you wonderful peace of mind to know that you are running to schedule and that everything will, therefore, get done in its turn. Try it for a while to see how it suits you: you could find that it really does help to keep you on course; ultimately, it will become second nature and you can discard the timetable, just making a new one if circumstances change. I recommend you still keep a written jobs list, though, especially for tasks that don't automatically need doing daily, then you can be sure you never forget anything, which is easy when you are busy.

time-savers and ease-makers

exercise

Ride and lead is a great way to cut riding time, provided your horses are trained for it and the riding environment is safe.

Rubber mats make a softer, safer and warmer floor for your horse. Bedding can be up to air the floor when the horse is out, but put it down whenever the horse is in.

UNFORTUNATELY FOR BUSY OWNERS, there is no substitute for physical activity for your horse. It stimulates just about every system in his body, strengthens him, supples him, calms his mind (believe it or not), satisfies him (as he is naturally a nomadic animal who, in the wild, would be gently on the move for many hours a day) and, when properly and sensibly done, along with correct feeding, is the main way of keeping him healthy and happy.

The only ways to save time on exercising horses are to turn them out, use a horsewalker, ride one horse and lead one or two, or get someone else to do it. It's that simple. Working a horse loose only saves the tacking up and untacking time – you still have to be there.

bedding

THE MOST TIME-SAVING bedding method is certainly deep litter. You can skip out and replenish bedding in a dozen boxes on deep litter in the time it takes to fully muck out one. However, deep litter is not very good for the horse (see p.47). Semi-deep litter, where droppings and the worst of the bedding are removed and replaced by clean material, is healthier. Working owners can follow a semi-deep litter routine during the week, and then do a full muck out at the weekend (see also pp.136–137).

THE BEST BARROWS AND BROOMS

Even if it costs a lot, a big wheelbarrow with an axle and two wheels is worth a lot as it is easy to handle and steer, and big enough for the one- or two-horse owner, it holds plenty and reduces trips to the muck heap. Small, single-wheeled barrows don't hold enough, necessitating several trips. They also tip over easily, and if you spill muck on the yard, even I admit that it's not acceptable to leave it there – making another job you can do without.

Choose wide-headed brooms as they sweep twice as much of the yard in each push. Synthetic bristles split and keep hold of the bedding whereas natural bristles don't, and they last longer, too.

grooming

Hot towelling (shown right)

1 You'll need two buckets of very hot water, thick rubber gloves and a couple of old terry towels.

*2 Soak a towel in the water and wring it out hard. Quickly fold it into a pad to keep the heat in and rub firmly and quickly **across** the lie of the hair to raise and remove dirt and grease. Refold the pad to a fresh, hot surface for each new part of the horse.*

3 Resoak the towel often.

4 Don't forget sensitive and private parts. Let the towel's surface cool a little first for these.

IT TAKES A FIT, experienced groom half an hour to thoroughly groom or strap a horse, longer if the horse is going to be wisped (or 'banged') as well. If properly done, full grooming stimulates the skin and superficial circulation, gives a general massage and establishes a relationship between horse and handler. However, if you are really short of time, full grooming can be substituted with a 'lick and a promise', such as a quick dandy brushing, followed by sponging both ends.

using both hands

When dandy brushing off mud and dried sweat, have a brush in each hand and go over the horse with quick, long strokes – left, right, left, right – occasionally scrubbing the bristle ends along each other (low down and away from the horse) to remove some dust and dirt.

For real speed when body brushing, try a trick I developed some years ago. Get a tough pair of leather chaps and two metal curry combs (the sort with a hand loop across the back). Using leather thonging or strong binder twine, fasten the curry combs – teeth running horizontally – to the chaps at the top and front of the thighs. Do this by passing the thonging or binder twine along the grooves between the metal teeth at the top end of the curry combs and into holes punched in the chaps. Tie the ends together firmly inside the chaps. Repeat at the bottom of each comb so they are both well fixed. Now take a body brush in each hand. Work quickly all over the horse giving long, firm strokes with alternate hands. After two or three strokes with each hand, clean the brushes by scraping them down the curry combs on your thighs, both at the same time. So, you are brushing like this: left, right, left, right, left, right, scrape, scrape, left, right, left, right, left, right, scrape, scrape! I know it sounds funny but it will cut your body brushing time by half.

quartering

This might constitute your lick and promise. Quartering the horse before exercise perks him up and makes him presentable. The point is to make sure

all areas touched by his tack are free from mud and dried sweat so that the skin is not rubbed sore.

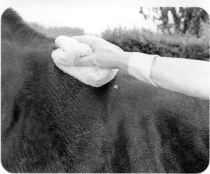

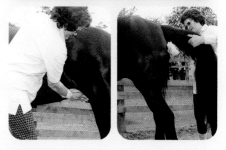

washing

Rinsing the horse off (not necessarily using soap or shampoo) really helps to keep him clean, weather permitting, and is quicker than grooming. When you would like to wash him but it is too cold, try hot towelling instead (see description top left and pictures above).

After washing, an infra-red lamp in your horse's box saves drying time and relaxes him (see p.76). They are fairly inexpensive.

coat dressings

Commercial dressings (usually spray-on) really do help repel dirt from the coat, mane and tail – it almost drops off as you groom. Spray-on shampoos can also be effective, if you find a good make, but they don't get right down to the skin.

time-saving equipment

not just a luxury

washing box It is relatively easy to organize a washing box or undercover area with a hosepipe for hosing down horses attached by a screw fitting to a mixer tap or instant heater that can be adjusted to give water at a variable temperature. Dousing people with cold water is a standard means of torture so why should horses be any different? Water at blood heat is kinder and more effective. You'll have no more chilled, miserable, reluctant and maybe resistant horses but clean, warm, contented ones who probably even enjoy their wash-down and, because they are warm, will dry off quicker than if they were thoughtlessly done with cold water.

heater box A heater box, or solarium, for drying is a real boon and saves time in rugging, leading round and so on. An infra-red heater in the roof is all that is needed, unless you want to splash out on an equine solarium. After washing you simply rough towel the horse's pasterns and heels and put him under the lamps with no rugs or blankets and plenty of ventilation, such as an open top door and window, plus a hay supply to keep him occupied and he will dry off quite quickly even with a long coat.

Never put a horse under a heater wearing a rug made of heat-retaining fabric as he may actually burn under it.

A washing area undercover or in a box is a big advantage for any yard.

Synthetic tack is much easier to care for than leather, which can be kept for best.

Right: Automatic drinkers, set at the horse's elbow height, are fine provided you check them regularly and they have a meter, so you can monitor how much your horse drinks.

tack Synthetic saddles are generally much cheaper than leather ones and can be used every day to save wear and tear on your best equipment. While synthetic tack is not as comfortable as leather, all else being equal, it does save lots of time on cleaning. You only need to rinse or wipe it down with a cloth or sponge and hot water. Many synthetic items have cheap metal fittings so it may be worth having decent buckles and so on attached at the time of purchase, if your supplier will do it.

Leather tack can be expensive, but usually gets more comfortable with age and is long-lasting, provided it is looked after well. Leather is sometimes treated with special finishes which mean not only that you do not need to clean it conventionally but actually that you must not do so for fear of ruining the finish. You can just wipe it over with a damp sponge. To save time on cleaning non-treated leather bridles, use warm water for the washing phase as this removes grease more easily, particularly if you put no more than a dash of washing-up liquid in the water.

other items Choose other equipment with care to save money and time. **Synthetic rugs and blankets** are easier to launder and dry quicker than natural fibres, but there's nothing so luxurious as the latter. Keep them for best. Follow manufacturers' laundering instructions or you could ruin the fabric.

Automatic drinkers save a lot of time and effort for owners and, when they work

properly, ensure that the horse always has water. However, some horses won't use certain types. Horses definitely drink more and most comfortably with their heads down, so ensure that your drinker is not above elbow height, at least, and preferably lower. Drinkers should be checked twice daily and have a drainage plug to facilitate cleaning out. The plumbing must be well lagged and protected if the system is not to freeze in hard weather. Some types have a meter so you know how much your horse has drunk, or otherwise: water intake is an indicator of general health or disorder, so an individual meter really is a good idea.

A telephone answering service really makes life easier, particularly on a commune-type yard (pp.56–63). Make checking it one of your first jobs on arriving at the yard. This way you know instantly if anyone can't make it to their horse, thereby ensuring that he will not be neglected or overlooked. Transfer all messages to the master diary (pp.82–85). Most phone companies now provide an answering service. If there is no clients' phone on your yard, ask for a payphone to be installed – not everyone has a mobile phone. If you leave messages by text or email (where these facilities are available), devise some system to ensure that they will be picked up and dealt with promptly.

it's YOUR life

adjusting a few attitudes

It's good family training to teach everyone to help each other – adults and youngsters!

IF, AFTER GOING THROUGH your horse chores minutely, you find that you still want more quality time with your horse, not to mention the other areas of your life, then you need to make some changes.

If your family is the outdated kind which still believes that one person is responsible for all the chores, re-educate them to help out. All but young children can keep their own rooms fairly clean and tidy. Spouses and partners need to accept that, like everyone else, you are entitled to your own interests in exchange for everything else you do.

frequent, extra school-runs to a bare minimum – or stop them completely.

Let your answering service or machine take calls when you're enjoying 'Me' time. To get rid of time and energy 'thieves' on the phone, train your dog to bark on silent command or have a recording of your doorbell, so you can pretend there's someone at the door and you have to go.

learn to say 'No!'...
Delegate as many unwanted tasks as possible to someone else. If they decline, say, 'I know *just* how you feel. So, I suppose it just won't get done, then.' Shrug, smile and walk away.

...but don't take it for an answer
When you're receiving regular 'Nos' or demands from anyone, don't waste time and effort reasoning with them. You can't reason with unreasonable people. Be pleasant and firm, withdraw specified privileges, 'rights', favours or services – and *stick to your guns*, otherwise you are teaching them that you are weak and can be trampled over.

Your time is your own, after all, and no one else's.

redress the balance
If no one volunteers to help, just allocate chores and responsibilities to capable family members and DON'T do them yourself, or only do those that affect you.

Keep burdens such as committee memberships, club secretaryships and

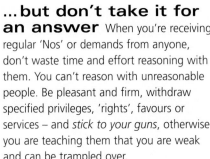

NOW ADJUST YOUR OWN ATTITUDE

Money is a poor criterion by which to value everything else. There's something wrong if the person who earns least (or nothing) is still working at bedtime while everyone else has been relaxing all evening. Is this you? If you have a feeling – even if it's no bigger than a pea – of anger, resentment and chaos inside you, remember that psychological stress (because that's what this is) can trigger potentially fatal cardiovascular, gastric and immune system diseases. Starting today, do something to help yourself.

1. If you feel permanently pressured, bad-tempered, tired and not particularly happy, you are either taking on too much or not working efficiently.

2. To manage your time effectively you have to get your priorities right (p.66).

3. Divide your horse jobs into As and Bs (see pp.68–69), the As being those that directly affect your horse and the Bs being those that don't. Never give Bs priority!

4. Give yourself a little less time than normal to do particular jobs and work quickly: that way, you can build up extra time for other things.

5. Fine tune your jobs – and your attitude towards them. When really rushed, only do absolute essentials and *never* feel guilty.

6. Use the double-handed method of grooming to halve the time taken (p.75).

7. Rinse down your horse in warm weather to save grooming time.

8. Choose synthetic tack, rugs and blankets to save on cleaning time.

9. Install automatic drinkers to save time and labour.

10. Take your share of pleasure and relaxation. Do not be a doormat for everyone else.

making time in short

6

Get Organized

Can you remember important points about your stable management or do you find yourself running things in a haphazard hit-and-miss way? Wouldn't it be wonderful never to be caught out – never to find that you can't go to a particular show or event because you didn't book the farrier in time and your horse's shoes are not in a fit condition, and never to look silly when your vet asks certain vital questions about your horse's work or diet and you are unable to answer accurately?

Busy people benefit tremendously from meticulous organization, but when you are *really* working flat out, it is often the one thing that goes by the board. If you feel you haven't time to sit down, or even stand up, and write a quick list of everything you need to do, *and* gulp down a coffee at the same time for that much-needed caffeine, this is just the time that being organized really pays its way.

Organization is a big part of time management. If you leave everything to chance and expect your overworked brain to remember all the bits and pieces that need doing, it won't – take it from one who's been there. Writing things down again helps greatly (see also pp.66–72). Albert Einstein, one of the greatest physicists the world has ever known, made innumerable lists and notes: he believed in keeping his brain clear so that his creative genius could flow without the pollution of mundane details.

> *Einstein was a member, with fellow geniuses, of a musical group. He was having trouble getting the rhythm of one piece and an exasperated colleague remarked: 'The trouble with you, Albert, is that you can't count! It goes like this – one, two, three, one, two, three …'*

So, whether you use a computer with equestrian software, a printed organizer, make up your own or rely on a simple diary and other notices and charts stuck up in the yard or barn, do try to create a system of some sort.

the master diary

setting up the diary

FAULTLESS ORGANIZATION IS EASY to achieve by creating your own personal planning system, which I call the 'master diary'. It can be adapted for use by individual owners or by communal groups, and runs like this:

❶ *Buy a diary (see left) and divide the pages horizontally into three equal sections.*

1) Action: *Things that must be done that day. List here vital jobs, such as order feed, post entries for Bumpton one-day event or buy a new spare wheel for the trailer.*

2) Your horse's day: *Include planned exercise, training, turn out and feeding regime. Rule this middle section vertically into three equal columns, the first for proposed exercise/turn out, the second for feed details and the third for remarks such as 'Bonnie left her second feed, sluggish at exercise, temperature 39°C'. This last gives a comprehensive record to guide you for the future or to show to your vet. When a horse falls ill or during a long illness, long-term records that include temperature, pulse, respiration, symptoms and general behaviour, including consumption of food and drink, can be vital.*

3) Actual: *Record what actually happened on that day. If everything went as planned, say so, but if not, put what did occur, such as 'Tansy sick, vet came pm…' plus details of treatment. Record diagnosis and precise treatment so that you have a proper record for future reference. Also use this section to note routine visits like 'farrier came pm, two new front, hind trimmed and reset, paid xxx' or 'delivery 12 bales bedding, paid xxx'.*

❷ *Once the diary is ruled up, first fill in the information you wrote on your year planner (p.29) – your holidays, major shows or events, and then minor ones. When your main occasions are filled in, your horse's fitness programme can be worked out backwards from the relevant dates. Also mark the dates of your horse's medicals (to be fitted round his work/holiday dates), vaccinations and boosters, dental checks, blood tests or profiles, or whatever is being done. If you are responsible for your land, record your grazing care schedule – land treatment and rotation plan, soil tests, dates to fertilize (when you fertilize remember to record which fertilizer you used and in what amounts).*

❸ *When you have done that, you can start filling in the action sections so you have everything prepared beforehand. For example, if you need the vet to visit on a particular date to do a blood test, put a note in the action section about two or three weeks before that date, so that you remember to book the vet well in advance. Note down the time of the appointment when you make it, too.*

❹ *Ask the vet to plan your horse's worming routine and doses, and again mark the appropriate dates, making a note a week before to buy the right drug in the right amount. If you have more than one horse, begin each entry with the horse's name so that you see at once to whom it relates. When similar regular tasks, such as shoeing, are carried out, record in the diary exactly what was done and the cost. In the case of the farrier, rebook him for, say, six weeks ahead when he is there, then put the appointment in the diary.*

❺ *At the end of the diary, record any special dates to be put into next year's diary, so that your programme carries on automatically. Buy a new diary as soon as they are in the shops so that your forward planning is not interrupted.*

ACTION

Order feed
Call Peter to remove muck heap
Collect wormers from Marsden's
● Ring Bob to replace Bunny's shoe
● Load trailer for Blanktown show tomorrow

BOOK ANNUAL VET. CHECKS
● REMEMBER JANE ON HOLIDAY FROM TOMORROW

● PAT: PLEASE TURN BUNNY OUT a.m.

● TIZZIE: 2hrs active hack	3 feeds as board OK	Very forward going
● TANSY: 1hr. school + jumping	3 " " " OK	Refusing oxer
● BUNNY: 1hr. hack, walk/trot	3 " " " Cut as no work	Lost shoe, turned out

ACTUAL

● Cut Tizzie's concentrates to 5lbs/2.5kg. Too lively!
Wormed all three with Brand Y.
● Bob arrived p.m., replaced Bunny's left hind shoe. Paid £XX
24 bales shavings arrived from Ainsworth's WRONG BRAND!
● Rang Kate to arrange lesson/school for Tansy. Left message
● Loaded trailer. Loose panel.

NOTES

● = Pat   ● = Jane   ● = Jill

the master diary

using the diary

IN A COMMUNAL YARD, get a diary with a hollow spine so you can thread some string down it and tie it to the table in the tack room, so that it never 'walks'. All owners can use it to enter when they are riding, when their horse should be done by someone else, when he should be turned out, and so on. Knowing what they are doing and when is very useful, enabling you to organize to share a vet's visit or have someone to hack out with, for example.

If you have several owners using the diary, these sorts of messages will need a separate section so you may need a two-pages-to-a-day diary.

Insist that all owners get into the habit of looking at the diary, not to mention filling it in, then there will be little chance of mix-ups, which could result in some poor horse being neglected.

card index

FOR A YARD of more than two or three horses, you might also find it useful to maintain a separate card index system for each horse for things like shoeing, worming and veterinary treatments, plus accidents and so on. You will then have a record by date in the diary and, in more detail, by individual horse on the index cards.

You can use the backs of the cards for fitness programmes and diet plus the dates of any major competitions attended. In this way, there is a ready record of each horse's management and activity available for vet, farrier and owner.

It is vital that you also keep careful records of your horse's registration numbers with different societies, including his security codes (freezemark, micro-chip number), his tack details and insurance policy numbers and the renewal dates of your own subscriptions to various clubs and societies.

Large yards will have separate shoeing records, and communes (p.58) should have a feed chart, the latter normally being marked up on a board in the feed room.

BACK-UP

With a regularly updated diary and card index system, necessary tasks, appointments and accurate records automatically unfold before you on a daily basis. The only problem is that you are sure to have a heart attack if you lose the diary. This is an excellent reason for keeping a back-up copy on a computer. It is, of course, essential that the two records are very closely co-ordinated and checked for accuracy to avoid mix-ups.

colour
coding

Alternating your paddocks is important for the health of your grazing, so put this in the diary, and make up a rota showing whose turn it is to pick up droppings.

INCREASE YOUR SEE-AT-A-GLANCE facility by using different coloured pens for different types of entry – for instance, red for veterinary and related topics such as first aid, vaccinations, worming and so on, orange for farriery, green for exercise, blue for competing, purple for feeding, brown for turn out, and so on. Alternatively, in communal yards, you could have a different colour pen for each owner so you can tell at once which entries relates to whom. To be really on the ball, you can use a loose-leaf ring binder instead of a bound diary and have pages of different colours for different owners or horses. These ideas can also be extended to the card index system, if you have one, and to feed charts. There is no limit to the variations.

Provided that you have remembered to write everything in as a matter of habit every day, there is only one thing you will ever have to remember and that is TO LOOK IN THE DIARY!

the tack room

essential facilities

TACK ROOMS NEED HEATING and/or air conditioning to keep the temperature at a reasonable level (room temperature is advised). Fabric and particularly leather soon deteriorates in very cold, very hot or damp surroundings. Ideally there should be both hot and cold running water: a kettle or an instant water heater over a sink. It is easier to clean grease off leather with slightly warm water; do not use hot water as it can spoil and discolour the hide.

In large yards, there may be washing machines and dryers in the tack room or a laundry room for rugs and blankets, saddle cloths, numnahs, jeans and working jodhpurs, fleeces and so on, but in smaller yards these will need to be dealt with by specialized laundries or at home. (See Security, pp.88–93, for tack room security considerations.)

To work efficiently for all its users, the tack room should have a readily accessible list of useful telephone numbers, such as veterinary

CLEANING

A saddle horse or stand with a reversible V-shaped top is great for cleaning saddles – right way up for the top of the saddle and upturned to rest it in to clean the underneath. You can fit a boot shelf underneath, and drawers in it can be used for tack-cleaning materials.

Bridles can be cleaned from a heavy bridle hook hanging from the ceiling provided you put it away after use, otherwise it might knock someone on the head.

practices (your usual, plus back-ups), farriers, club and hunt secretaries, saddlers, feed merchants and so on. It could also include numbers for complementary therapists, teachers, professional clippers, freelance grooms, transporters, car mechanics and tack stores. All owners' day, evening and mobile numbers should be on this list as well as on the index cards, so there is a double record.

Although tidying the tack room may be a B-list job (p.69), there is a limit to the amount of chaos that should be allowed, especially as some users will be messier than others. Reasonable cleanliness and tidiness are more pleasant than grunge and ensure that important things like first aid kits are immediately to hand. Individual owners are sure to want their own veterinary supplies and like their own preferred brands or those recommended by their particular veterinary practice. However, emergency first aid supplies could be bought out of the kitty budget.

FIRST AID

Veterinary supplies must be kept up-to-date, clean and available as correct first aid can help or hamper future treatment. Reserve a clean cupboard for veterinary and similar supplies, and put a list on the back of the door stating what is in there. If any item is running low, it should be noted and replaced before it runs out.

A good up-to-date veterinary book should be kept in there, ideally tied so that it can be referred to but not removed.

A good first aid kit for humans is also an essential, along with an up-to-date first aid manual. It is well worth having at least one qualified first aider – perhaps a different owner could go on a course each year.

storage

EACH OWNER SHOULD KNOW where in the tack room communal things are stored and, ideally, have their own section for tack and equipment. In a large yard there will need to be storage chests or cupboards for clothing, drawers for boots and bandages and shelves for all the clutter that gravitates to tack rooms. Old lockers, shelves, chest freezers, kitchen cabinets and so on can all be used efficiently and cheaply. Racks for rugs and blankets can be made for nothing out of brush handles and baler twine. An old-fashioned clothes rack with four or more wooden or plastic poles hauled above head height on a pulley is really useful if the ceiling is strong and high enough. Saddle and bridle storage should be plentiful and can be bought or made cheaply. A wooden bracket shaped like an upturned V, floor-standing or wall-mounted, is good for saddles, which should never be stored on poles or ropes as this can stretch the seat from underneath. Bridles and leather headcollars should be stored on rounded holders so that the headpieces keep their shape and do not become ridged and cracked as they would if hung on a narrow wooden peg or nail; old saddle-soap tins or semi-circles of wood nailed to the wall are ideal for this.

tack room checklist

1 Ample storage for tack, clothing, up-to-date veterinary supplies and an up-to-date vet book, and other equipment, communal or individual.

2 Saddle horse and bridle hook, if possible, to facilitate easy tack cleaning.

3 Heating/air conditioning and a thermostat to maintain the atmosphere at a constant (room) temperature for the preservation of tack.

4 Good ventilation is needed as humidity from wet jobs and boiling kettles create a damp, unpleasant and potentially damaging atmosphere.

5 Each owner will appreciate having their own bay or section for their belongings, with a locker, trunk or cupboard for storage. Most people prefer something lockable.

6 Choose a prominent site to display a list of owners' and other useful phone numbers.

7 Have a notice displayed saying *Don't put it down – put it away.* This should help maintain tidiness and order without tidying up becoming a specific job.

8 The master diary and supporting card index can be kept in here on a table ready for everyone to refer to and use.

9 Hot and cold water, ideally running. Hot and cold drinks facilities are always welcome – an instant water heater over a large sink or a kettle will fill the bill.

10 Toilet facilities, even if only of the chemical sort, really should be available.

security

tack and tack rooms

MOST THIEVES AND VANDALS are opportunists, tending to go for places which offer easy pickings, but we must accept that determined thieves can get into almost anywhere so the best we can do is make life as difficult for them as possible with effective security measures.

Not all yards have adequate precautions for tack, and insurance companies have strict requirements on security arrangements. Some will not cover tack if it is not kept in the owner's house or if the siting, structure and security of the tack room are not up to their specified standards. Many horse owners in communal stables prefer to take at least their saddle home with them for safety's sake. There is a booming trade in stolen tack because it is so expensive, and so good precautions are worthwhile.

Various security companies, most working in co-operation with the police, will code tack and keep a register of the codes (look for their adverts in horse magazines). If you prefer to go it alone, you can mark your tack yourself with any of the methods approved by your local police force, from indelible inks and markers to embossing or stamping. A visible mark is more of a deterrent to thieves than one that can only be detected by a scanner. In Britain it is advised that you use your postcode plus your house number or the first three letters

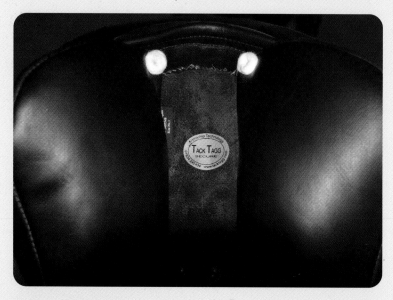

Security lights are an excellent deterrent to thieves and vandals, most of whom prefer to hide under cover of darkness. However, lights should be high up so that they cannot easily be put out of action by intruders.

Security stamping your saddle is another good way of deterring thieves – altered code numbers are usually quite obvious.

of its name. However, if you move home this can be very inconvenient as everything has to be remarked. A better number, if longer, is your National Insurance ID, which is yours for life.

design and site
The siting and construction of your tack room can be very relevant to its security. If possible, it's always safer to have it attached to living quarters as it is less likely to become a target. A brick, block or stone building is stronger than timber. Door and window frames must be very strongly fixed to the walls, with unbreakable or reinforced glass or PVC used for windows and key-operated locks fitted. Doors should be fitted with at least one five-element mortice lock.

Do *not* put a notice on the tack room door announcing its presence for the benefit of intruders. Any cupboards within the room should be kept locked, too.

horses and ponies

FEW THINGS CAN BE more heartbreaking than having a much-loved horse or pony stolen. Fortunately, freeze-marking and/or micro-chipping are common and are excellent deterrents to thieves. Most

cold irons are held against the skin for long enough to kill the colouring pigment so that the hair that regrows is white. Grey or white horses have the irons held on longer to completely kill hair growth there.

Micro-chips are inserted in the crest of the neck by means of a 'gun' which inserts a chip the size of a grain of rice under the skin. Police, veterinary practices, horse sales and abbatoirs have electronic scanners to reveal the number, which is then checked with national registries.

Hoof-branding usually involves your postcode or zip code being burned onto your horse's hooves. It is done by your farrier and is redone as the horn grows down. Your farrier should have details of registries.

If you plan to use a commercial marking company, ask around before making a selection, read their conditions very carefully and be prepared to comply with them to the letter as some are otherwise disappointingly poor at helping in recovery or in paying out rewards. Some companies require you to tell them first if your horse goes missing, before informing even the police, some require written confirmation, some are helpful, while others expect you to do everything yourself.

Freeze-marking is an excellent way of helping to keep your horse safe from thieves. This horse is marked on the shoulder; it is more common to place the mark on the saddle area.

companies that offer the service work closely with the police and usually offer fairly high rewards for information leading to the recovery of an animal.

A horse is freeze-marked, usually on the saddle area, with an individual code. Super-

EQUINE PASSPORTS

In European Union member countries it is now a legal requirement for all equines to have passports, which are a combination of identity and veterinary records. The passport contains a diagram, similar to a veterinary certificate, showing identifying colourings and other marks plus a record of the administration of specified drugs. This should enable horses and horse carcasses to be accurately identified. The reason for this legislation is to safeguard the health of any person eating a slaughtered equine and to prevent certain drugs entering the human food chain. As horses are used for food in many parts of mainland Europe, this precaution is understandable. Drugs-treated animals can be euthanased by captive bolt ('shooting') or by lethal injection. Non drugs-treated animals can also be euthanased by either method, but the use of a lethal injection means that the carcass cannot be used for human consumption.

In Britain, the carcasses of drugs-treated animals are now cremated and the ashes disposed of in a land-fill site. It is no longer possible for an owner to have the ashes of their horse returned to them for retention or burial.

vandals and joy-riders

THERE IS AN INCREASE in the number of attacks on horses today. These seem senseless and motiveless to normal people but others clearly get pleasure and satisfaction out of causing great suffering, distress and even death as a result of vandalism, joy-riding horses to exhaustion and stabbings. Often affected horses are abandoned loose or not even removed from their premises.

The security of all places where horses are kept is vital. Animals most at risk are those in isolated fields with easy access but away from homes and other buildings, and those stabled (easy access again) in yards where there is little security or human presence.

All horses should be checked daily for injuries or signs of any interference such as wounds, rugs having been removed and replaced, also unusual behaviour like nervousness or unusual quietness. Anything suspicious should be reported to your vet, and usually to the police, as well, without delay.

Don't forget to keep other valuable items safe from thieves. There is a ready market in stolen trailers so a wheel clamp is a worthwhile investment.

EQUINE IDENTITY PACK

Make an identity pack for immediate distribution to regional or national sales, dealers, slaughterers, the press (not only equestrian) and the police – make a list of phone numbers and addresses so that they are readily to hand if you need them. You will need to include clear colour snapshots of your horse from both sides, front and back, with close-ups of any distinguishing marks including scars, hair whorls and his freezemark, plus his four chestnuts, which are as individual to horses as our fingerprints are to us. Keep the photographs up-to-date as his appearance will change when he is clipped and grey horses grow lighter, for example. Make sure you have enough copies of your identity pack to send immediately to everyone on your list. You could also put a pack on computer for emailing where it is possible.

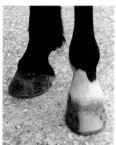

security

increasing deterrents

Thick, overgrown field edges, complicated paddock layouts and only one main, very secure gate on to a public road, combine to make life difficult for thieves. Anything that will add to their problems and confusion will help keep your horses safer.

LOCAL POLICE USUALLY HAVE crime prevention departments and will send an officer to your yard to advise you on your risks and what is best to do about them. They can recommend products and measures to deter intruders. I have found that they have a practical outlook and will recommend the most reasonably-priced equipment that is effective enough to do the job. You can consider intruder alarms, security sensor lights, cameras and closed-circuit TV.

Thick, high, prickly hedging is more off-putting than wooden or wire fencing, which intruders can easily cut or saw through, although they may drive vehicles through almost anything. If it is practical, plant hedging across all gates on the outer perimeter of your property except for your main entrance. Have gates opening into your property and not on to a public road or track, and make sure that they cannot be lifted off their hinges. Consider fitting sensors to them and around the perimeters of your property or at least an inner ring, if it is a big place. Padbars (bolts that can take a padlock) with heavyweight padlocks are more effective than chains (unless of hardened metal) and should be fitted to both ends of gates. Use these all around your buildings. Ideally, no building should back on to a road, private or public, as this gives easy access for thieves to break through walls.

On communal yards, have a notice stating that all visitors must report straight to the office or house, *not* the tack room for obvious reasons. Anyone found wandering about should be approached and escorted to the reception area, however informal.

Turning out horses in headcollars makes it easy for thieves to catch and lead them. It is safer for those that are out at night to be brought into home paddocks ringed by sensors than left in outlying fields. Guard dogs must be tethered and geese and other aggressive animals may be found 'guilty' of attacking intruders, to the cost of their

owners. Permitted security fencing materials and heights are no longer very effective so hedges are among the best security measures available at present. The tougher, higher, thicker and pricklier they can be grown, the better. Taking advice from the police about improving your security

measures and warning notices is strongly advised if you do not wish to receive a compensation claim from any intruder who hurts themselves when entering your property. On the plus side, any kind of neighbourhood watch scheme is well worth implementing. Also keep friendly with your neighbours and ask them to tell you of anyone loitering around your place, and be prepared to return the favour.

MAKE IT CLEAR

It is worth having notices around your property, warning intruders to keep out and stating that security measures are in place. I have been told that this will also reduce the compensation you pay if an intruder is hurt on your premises.

stable and yard layout

shelter and air circulation

MOST OF US have little choice over our yard layout, particularly if we keep our horses at livery or in rented accommodation. Where there is choice, or permission to change things, a little thought about how the buildings and general facilities are arranged can save a lot of time and work.

Stable yards should be sited so that they are in neither an airless, humid spot nor exposed to prevailing winds. Shelter should be on the side of the yard from which the coldest winds blow, to the north and east in Britain and Ireland. Shelter belts such as trees or close-woven plastic mesh help break the wind rather than blocking it. Reasonable air circulation aids in reducing the development and spread of disease and very sheltered yards can feel oppressive in summer.

In a line of conventional loose boxes or stalls, it helps to have an overhang roughly 2m (6ft) wide to protect the horses from extremes of weather, and stables should be designed so that a cross-draught above

head height can be created for adequate air change, by means of windows opposite the door, louvres in all walls and so on. Even just removing a plank or two or a few bricks here and there helps. It is normally advised that boxes face south in the northern hemisphere but an extra lookout point in a back or side wall can help airflow, and horses feel safer when they can look about them freely.

SIZE DOES MATTER!

Research has indicated that a 16hh horse needs a stable about 5m (17ft) square to provide adequate physical space and peace of mind. This is well beyond the reach of most owners but the minimum for a horse of that height should be 3.7m (12ft) square. Horses also like plenty of headroom – aim at 3.6m (11ft) to the eaves wherever possible, more in a single-planed roof.

American barn-type stabling can be convenient for people but horses may suffer from darkness and lack of fresh air. In this one, the horses cannot even look out of their stables.

Yarding is a good system of housing horses and should be used much more. These horses are quite happy in their roomy, well ventilated covered yard. The doors at the bottom can be left open or closed either to keep the horses in or allow them out onto pasture.

american barns This style of barn was originally devised for extremes of temperature and weather as it provides protection for horses and humans nearly all the time. It is basically a barn with wide doors at both ends and the boxes sited down the outside walls, although some have a passageway or shedrow inside the perimeter wall for exercising. The central aisle is wide enough to allow a tractor or horse and trailer (no pollution) to pass down, delivering feed or removing manure. These barns usually have one short end to the prevailing wind so that in summer, with the doors propped open, a breeze can blow down the length of the barn but in winter, with the doors closed, a small area is presented to the winds, reducing their overall chilling effect. Extra ventilation points should still be provided.

yarding Where yards have shelter sheds, filling up communal hayracks is much easier through hatches opening on the walls to the outside. This way attendants can replenish the racks without being waylaid by a gang of hungry horses.

Yards with shelters can often be made to continue on into the grassland, avoiding the need for a shelter out there as well. Horses can go from the yard or shed, perhaps on to a surfaced area (which can be fenced off if it is required to keep the horses off grass) and then out to the grass, as they wish. It saves time and walking if humans have access into the shed from the stable yard.

In linked fields, one simple shelter can be made to serve three paddocks or more by siting it at their junction. The same goes for watering points. Such shelters will have to be skipped out and stocked up with hay and perhaps bedding and the horses regularly caught and inspected, so it is convenient and time-saving to have them, and water containers, as near as is reasonably possible to the yard to cut down distances for carting hay, bedding and other gear to and fro.

'Use your head to save your legs!'
This saying came from my father who meant that by having everything conveniently sited, you use less time and energy walking from place to place. It helps if small feed stores and tack rooms can be placed at, say, every sixth box, indoors or out.

examples of yard layouts

This shows one end of a covered barn which has been adapted as a covered yard with direct access to a paddock. Hay is supplied in the hayracks around the perimeter of the barn. This facility provides for the horses' physical and mental needs.

This shows ideal facilities for yards large or small. The play area in the foreground has been drained so it is usable in all seasons. The shelter has a deep-litter bed and haynets and a door at the back for easy access for the owners. By leaving the field gate open, the horses can come and go into the pasture as they please or access can be restricted in bad conditions.

This field shelter is sited on the highest and therefore driest part of the field with its back to the prevailing wind. The hayrack is kept stocked up except when grazing is plentiful. A gutter and downpipe carry away rain water which would otherwise drop onto the horses who tend to stand half-in and half-out of the shelter.

Almost anything is preferable to being stabled all the time – here two former bull boxes with their pens in front have been converted successfully for horse use.

This housing was previously used for young cattle. The wooden hayracks give large communal supplies of hay which can be reached on both sides and the animals can see each other increasing their sense of company. This sort of stabling is suitable for housing several temperamentally compatible animals in one box.

proper storage

Spring weighers for hay are available from most good saddleries and feed merchants and are worth using, especially if your horse is on a controlled diet.

IF IT IS TO KEEP WELL, feed of all kinds must be stored properly. Whether indoors, outdoors or half-and-half in an open-sided barn, hay should be stored off the ground, although this may be difficult for large quantities. Wooden pallets are sometimes used for fairly small quantities. However, these allow rats to get underneath without being high enough to let a cat or terrier get in to root them out. A reasonable height is 30cm (12in), if this can be arranged. New hay should be stacked with space between the bales to allow it to 'breathe'.

The feed room should have a dry atmosphere and should be swept out as often as possible to avoid spilled food not only attracting rats and mice any more than is inevitable, but also to prevent its developing mouldy growth and encouraging bacteria. Hot, running water is an advantage for making warm, damped feeds and cleaning containers after each feed. Oils and sticky substances are more effectively removed with warm or hot water than cold. If cooked feeds are used, a boiler will be required in a large establishment for barley, whole oats or linseed, or a hotplate in a small one. If your yard cannot supply such a facility, you can always bring your own cooked feed from home in a large vacuum flask or insulated picnic container.

Feed storage bins, of whatever type, need some indication on the outside of the type of feed they hold. This will speed up making up feeds and saves you having to check each bin to see what it holds on the next delivery.

Even if the feed is tipped into his manger, each horse should have his own bucket, with his name on it, to help minimize the spread of disease. This also ensures there are no mix-ups if other people are doing the feeding. Where horses may be fed by people not completely familiar with their diets, a large wipe-clean board is perfect for writing up rations for quick and easy reference; any changes must be inserted promptly and accurately.

weigh it! Much feed is wasted and many horses over or under fed because their feed is not weighed properly. It pays from both an economic and health point of view to have a method of weighing grain and concentrates such as coarse mixes or nuts. A large kitchen scale is quite adequate. Alternatively, use a measure with the amount by weight of each feed it holds clearly written on it, so there is no guessing.

Hay or haylage should also be weighed. If haynets are used, it is a simple matter to hang each net on a simple spring weigher, available from most tack suppliers or the better agricultural merchants. If it is fed in racks or loose, weigh it by placing it on an opened-out sack, bringing the four corners together and hooking them on the weigher. The forage can be carried to the stable in the same sack to help prevent bits blowing about the yard.

DELIVERING THE GOODS

When feeding several animals, it is easier to cart the haynets, buckets or other containers to the stables on a trolley or flat trailer. It's not very pleasant to use a muck barrow so you might feel it's worth buying a separate one for feeds.

On larger yards, or smaller ones where one person does the horses, feeding is made quicker by means of a small door with the manger attached to it on the outer wall: this can be opened from the outside and the feed just tipped in. It may not sound very time-saving but it is when you have a lot of horses to feed.

1. A master diary system never crashes nor do its batteries fail, and everyone can grasp how to use it. It is the life-support system of your stable, from a small private one to a communal set-up.

2. A supporting card index system for individual horses is a refinement for larger yards.

3. Read the tack room checklist on p.87.

4. Call your local police crime prevention department to assess your premises for reasonably priced and practical security measures. All tack should be marked and horses and ponies freezemarked and/or micro-chipped.

5. Make an identity pack for distribution to the press, slaughterers, sales, dealers and others, should your horse be stolen.

6. Report cases of vandalism to your horse to your vet and the police.

7. Badly stored feed is often spoiled and wasted.

8. Weigh feed so you are sure of your horse's ration; this avoids over/under feeding and waste.

9. Give your horse the roomiest stable you can find, all else being equal; horses are happiest with plenty of space and, most importantly, a good view out of their stable, so an extra viewpoint is usually much appreciated. Strive for good ventilation without draughts.

10. Yarded horses save a lot of time, money and effort: it's a brilliant alternative to individual stabling.

Care in a Nutshell

It is fine to cut corners, but only if you know exactly where to cut them without harming your horse or compromising his welfare. To do this, you need to be a knowledgeable horsemaster. Advising novices to cut down on certain tasks could lead to important areas of management being skimped due to lack of understanding. It is like learning to recognize injury or illness in a horse: we need to know what is normal before we can see what is abnormal. This section is an overall guide to caring for horses well, but still with an eye to saving time and money.

The days are long gone when yards could provide one groom per two horses. The economies of horse keeping in the early twenty-first century preclude the continuance of many of the practices devised by employers and horsekeepers of the nineteenth and even twentieth centuries, but some of these methods live on in present-day textbooks and in establishments where finance isn't a problem. For most horse owners, however, there simply isn't the time and money to perform them and, fortunately for anyone who hasn't all day to devote to a horse or two, there are many that can be safely skimped or skipped without any harm to the horse.

What appears here inevitably comprises my own views, formed from my knowledge and opinions on horse management, gained over a lifetime of hands-on experience, observation and personal and formal study. Some of the ideas and methods I recommend may seem like sacrilege to purists and traditionalists but they have withstood many years of practice with no detriment to the many different types of horses and ponies involved.

mind and body

satisfying his basic needs

Lack of liberty can have a very adverse effect on a horse's contentment and behaviour. Even a few hours out daily can satisfy his need to gallop and kick about and roll freely.

AS WE ALL KNOW, the horse is a herd animal of the wide open spaces. Most equines do not do well – mentally or physically – when living alone or over-confined. Horses have a natural love of and need for space, shelter, company, movement and an all-round view; life in a stable is clearly highly unnatural to them and too much of it certainly causes problems. However, we all know of horses who want to be inside (in stable or shelter) sometimes and are reasonably content, provided they can see and preferably touch other horses, have constant fibre to eat and water to drink and ground conditions on which they are happy to stale and lie down.

Most of the stable vices normally blamed on boredom are due to the distress of over-confinement and other stressful factors such as lack of company and something to eat, uncomfortable rugs or blankets and unsuitable surfaces on which to stale or lie. Improved management always results in horses becoming healthier and happier and much easier and pleasanter to look after and work with.

turn out is vital

A HORSE'S TURNING OUT period is of equal importance to other daily requirements. They may enjoy their work and many feel left out when not in work but exercise under constraint is no substitute for liberty. Far too many owners and yard managers overlook or blatantly ignore horses' needs in this respect, even though they are so easily fulfilled: all they require is to be turned out, preferably into a grass paddock, for as long as possible each day, and allowed freedom in the company of their friends and the chance to do the things horses need to do.

The provision of liberty requires adequate facilities but this is not beyond the means of most yards, using a little imagination and willingness. If grassed areas are not available, horses can be put in a riding arena or other surfaced area with ample hay and water. Most yards have the odd, unused patch of ground or could sacrifice

a space – preferably adjoining a loose box or with a shed in it – that could be fenced off as a play area. Even in a small space, two friends can be turned out together and will exercise and be company for each other. Make sure that you sort out the ground surface of any such play area so that it is safe to lie and roll on, which is so important to horses. An earth or grass patch can be left as it is, unless very poorly drained, but harder areas will need attention. Such a facility is a real boon to any stables but particularly to a working owner short of time for exercising or who simply takes the right-minded view that horses are saner and happier with as much freedom as is reasonably possible. Their beds are saved, too, meaning less work and expenditure.

Of course, even hardy types are not happy in an exposed field for long periods with no real protection from the elements, especially if they are alone. In truly natural conditions, animals have the chance to find shelter: trees and shrubbery, hills and hedges, woods and buildings all help to break the worst force of the weather and offer some shade in summer.

It is, therefore, an advantage to the horse and his busy owner if a little thought can be applied to the subject of facilities for liberty, and providing company is equally important (see box, below).

SOCIAL CONTACT

Natural social contact is much more important than many owners seem or wish to acknowledge. Horses feel more secure in the company of their own kind. In the wild, when they were subject to predators, there was safety in numbers – if there are lots of you, the predator may well pick someone else for dinner. This need for company is very strong, and although some horses do seem to survive contentedly (or resignedly) alone, my experience is that they become much happier when given company.

safe and sound

GOOD SECURE BOUNDARIES are vital wherever there are horses. It is worth making them sturdy and long-lasting, even if it costs a little more, and it is essential that you make them horseproof and horse-safe. Once they are in place, fences need very little regular maintenance, while hedges will need annual cutting, which can usually be carried out by a local farmer. Whatever your expenditure on hedges or fences, they are an indispensable facility to enable your horse to be turned out, easing your time and work burden.

hedging   Some kind of structure to contain horses is essential, and hedges, ideally thick, high, prickly ones, are traditionally used in Britain and Ireland and regarded as the best way of keeping horses in their place. Innovative horse owners in areas where hedges are uncommon could not only save themselves a lot of time and money in the long-term but also greatly help wildlife and the environment by growing hedges of native shrubs and trees. Hedges of this sort provide a habitat and food and a highway system for animals and birds, enabling them to move around their area safely and giving them a better chance of survival in areas where their habitat is threatened (which is most).

Ponies, sheep and cattle push through hedges, but horses jump over them, so they must be dense and, ultimately, at least as high as the horses' backs and preferably higher, certainly for stallions. A good hedge cannot be produced from scratch in less than a matter of years but if the land is your own or on a long lease it certainly pays to encourage the growth of non-toxic trees and shrubs along field boundaries. Once mature, hedges need trimming (not butchering) about once a year to encourage thick, healthy growth all the way through, and having the hedge professionally laid occasionally keeps it stockproof. Laying can be done by commercial firms, local conservation volunteers or college students looking for a project. It is better – from a conservation and maintenance viewpoint – to trim hedges into a flat-topped A-shape

so that they are deeper front to back at the bottom than the top. This allows the sun's rays to reach more of the leaves, which can then photosynthesize more easily and make their own food, so the hedge will flourish.

High, thick hedges are also an excellent security feature, hiding from general view what is on the other side and proving more impenetrable to intruders than most fences. They make valuable windbreaks and, if cultivated on all sides of your paddocks, provide some shade for the horses in summer through most of the day, although they can never take the place of overhead shelter.

fencing   The traditional fencing system for paddocks is **timber posts and rails**. This is expensive today but worthwhile, both aesthetically and practically, if you can afford it, and economies can be made. For mature horses, two-rail fencing is fine with the top rail at horse's back height and the next about halfway between it and the ground. On studs, three- and four-rail fencing is

Above: Natural hedges on at least the windward side of a field provide some shelter.

Right: Diamond mesh fencing is very effective and safe but rather expensive.

Far right: Flexible rail fencing is long-lasting and even a single line inside unsafe or broken fencing can make an unusable paddock available.

Electric fencing is really useful for dividing paddocks, reinforcing dubious fencing or protecting horses from barbed wire.

BARBED WIRE

No true horseman would dream of using barbed wire near horses. It is just too dangerous.

needed to stop foals getting through or rolling near the fence and ending up, panic stricken, away from Mum on the other side. In such cases, the bottom rail should be about 30cm (12in) from the ground.

Much cheaper and quite effective is **plain, heavy-gauge wire** strained tightly on wooden posts. Should one strand give way, though, it will sag along its whole length, lowering the fence if it is the top strand or causing a dangerous loop if lower. With shod horses, there is also some chance that a wire could become caught between the heel of the shoe and the hoof; this may terrify a horse and it can seriously injure itself struggling to get free. Wire clippers should always be kept where everyone knows they can find them in an emergency – somewhere in the tack room is ideal.

Diamond **mesh fencing** is good and horse-friendly but expensive. Square or rectangular mesh fencing is widely used; it must be of the type specially for horses with small mesh so that they cannot possibly get their feet through it.

Flexible-rail fencing, sometimes wire-reinforced, is effective and hard-wearing

although horses like to chew some types. One big advantage of this is that an owner using rented accommodation can use it as a top rail to patch up poor fencing but take it away when he or she moves the horse.

Electric fencing is now normally of the white tape or rope sort, which is really easy to erect, fully portable, cheap and long-lasting. You need access to a mains electricity supply although a heavy-duty battery may be used with some types. Electric fencing should not be the only barrier between the horse and the outside world, although it is fine for dividing up a large paddock or reinforcing a perimeter fence.

Rails or wire should be on the inside – field side – of the fencing posts so as to present as smooth a barrier as possible to galloping horses, preventing them from sustaining injuries on the posts. If a single fence separates two fields, one rail or wire at point-of-shoulder height should be run on the side on which the posts are exposed. Ideally, corners should be rounded off or have a rail set across them to steer galloping horses around them, not into them.

the digestive system

WHEN HORSES ARE ABLE to graze at leisure they tend to spend about 16 hours a day doing so. Like most herbivores, their natural food is fibrous, bulky and lower in nutrients than concentrated food such as meat, so to obtain enough nourishment from it, they have evolved to eat more or less continuously and always have some food passing through their digestive tract, unlike carnivores, for example, which can eat much less frequently.

Horses evolved to cope with grass more easily than any other feed.

The front teeth (incisors) crop off grass and leaves and the grinding teeth (premolars and molars) at the back of the jaw crush it up. The tongue and cheeks mix it with alkaline saliva to soften it.

stomach The stomach works best when it is about two-thirds full, including feed and digestive juices. Acid stomach juices start the process of breaking down the food, which then passes into the gut, a long, compartmentalized tube with muscular walls that push the food along in a wave-like movement called peristalsis. Starch from concentrates is absorbed into the bloodstream through the gut wall, mainly in the small intestine after the stomach. The food continues into the capacious large intestine, where fibre is mainly processed by microscopic organisms. The nutrients made available by this are absorbed into the bloodstream and then used by the parts of the body needing them. Some excess nutrients and food are stored for future use.

liver The liver filters the blood and helps to protect the body against unwanted substances. When potent poisons, such as those in ragwort, are eaten, the liver may become seriously damaged, affecting its many other functions and causing serious illness or death.

energy and fat Excess nutrients are stored in depots around the body, some as glycogen, which creates energy, and some as fat. The more food that is stored, the fatter the horse becomes. Horses with too little to eat lose fat, then muscle – hence the descriptive phrase 'skin and bone'– and eventually become emaciated. If a horse becomes so thin that he is using up his own body tissues, all other requirements are affected; there is simply not enough fuel to keep the body going and death can result. Conversely, when too much food is eaten, the horse will not only become fat but may develop serious circulatory, digestive and metabolic disorders such as colic, lymphangitis, laminitis and azoturia.

USES OF FOOD

- *Making body tissue such as muscle, skin, bone, horn and so on.*
- *Maintaining the body temperature at around 38°C (100.4°F).*
- *Putting on condition/weight (storage of food).*
- *Providing energy for work and body functions, including digestion itself.*

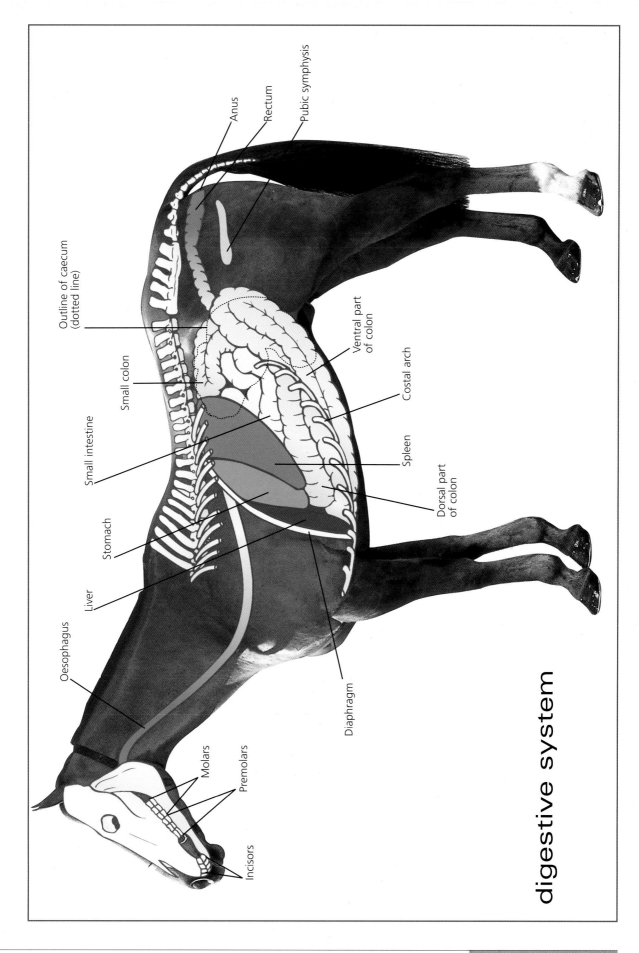

digestive system

Anus

Rectum

Pubic symphysis

Outline of caecum (dotted line)

Ventral part of colon

Small colon

Costal arch

Small intestine

Spleen

Dorsal part of colon

Stomach

Liver

Diaphragm

Oesophagus

Molars

Premolars

Incisors

what makes feed?

water

THE MAIN CONSTITUENTS of feed are: water, carbohydrates, proteins, fats, vitamins, minerals and trace elements.

Fresh water is, with air and sunlight, the world's most vital resource. We can survive much longer without food than we can without water. Dehydration, which is a potentially fatal condition, can occur in horses as easily when water sources freeze in winter as it can in summer, when they may dry up or the horse is working hard and sweating copiously, especially in hot weather.

A horse's body is about 70 per cent water. The cells are surrounded by and contain water-based fluids. Blood and lymph (a fluid that supports blood) are mainly water, as are digestive juices; the eyes and ears contain liquid, and the horse's joints are lubricated by a fluid called synovia. Mares use water to make milk and the horse's excretory system depends on water – urine transports waste and excess substances out of the body, droppings are moist and sweat contains waste products, too. Sweat is important in regulating temperature as heat is lost by its evaporation into the drier air.

WATER WISE

If you water your horse outside his stable, do not take him away from his source when he first lifts his head. He may well be resting, and will then have another drink. So, to ensure that he has had his fill, let him move away from the water of his own accord.

All the normal feeds contain some water but an additional source is essential. Horses and ponies can need to drink anything from 27 to 68 litres (6 to 15 gallons) a day, depending on their size and work and the weather.

drinking habits
Wild and feral equines normally drink early morning and evening, often trekking long distances to water. Years ago, domestic horses were watered morning and night only, although sometimes before feeding, too. The old rule was to water horses before and not after feeding so that feed was not washed on out of the stomach. Modern knowledge, however, confirms that ensuring horses have a continuous supply of water is beneficial as digestion is improved if they are allowed to drink a little before, during and after eating. Horses who always have water with them do not take long draughts unless after long, hot work.

CHECKING FOR DEHYDRATION

*There are two practical tests for detecting dehydration. The well-known **skin pinch test** involves pinching up and carefully twisting a fold of skin just in front of the shoulder. It should fall back flat more or less immediately, although some authorities say that a couple of seconds is acceptable. If it takes longer than this the horse is already significantly dehydrated.*

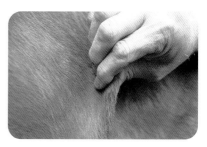

*The other which gives earlier warning, is the **capillary refill test**. With your thumb, press firmly on the gum just above one of the corner teeth – this will leave a pale patch. If the patch does not return to its normal salmon pink within two seconds the horse is dehydrated.*

A large, wide tub or bin, like this, secured to the fence and filled by tap or hosepipe is a good water source, although if water is laid on, as here, you might as well get a self-filling trough.

what makes feed?

water sources checklist

1 However you get it to the horse, the water supply needs checking at least twice daily for amount, cleanliness and safety.

2 Mains water can usually be relied upon to be safe but not always and it's worthwhile having periodic checks made, perhaps via your veterinary practice.

3 Natural water sources can easily become contaminated and cause illness, and must be checked very regularly. It may be better, for example, to fence off stagnant ponds or regularly polluted streams, and provide mains water instead – where there is no supply, transport water in bowsers or other large containers. In addition, steep-sided ponds or those that are frozen in winter are very dangerous as horses can fall in and be unable to get out again.

4 The best automatic drinkers for stables have plug holes for easy cleaning and meters so that the amount drunk, or not, can be monitored.

5 In stables, try to have two containers in different corners so that if the horse dirties one, he has an alternative. Always have the containers in the same places so that he knows where they are. Buckets or larger tubs are fine on the stable floor, perhaps tied or clipped to some support or placed inside an old car tyre to prevent the horse tipping them over.

6 The rim of the water container should not be higher than a horse's elbow height as horses need to drink (and eat) from a low source.

7 Small containers need daily scrubbing and rinsing out, as when they are slimy and dirty, they put off many horses and can encourage disease. Field troughs are normally cleaned less frequently for practical reasons.

8 In the field, moveable sources can be set at different points daily to prevent the ground around them becoming very muddy and trampled.

9 In fields where piped water is unavailable, plastic dustbins rammed into large tyres and tied to fence posts are a good, cheap alternative. Filled by hosepipe, they are quite convenient but keep the water level high as some horses don't like putting their heads deep down inside a container. Remember to bring the hose indoors in frosty weather as if it freezes you will have no water supply.

10 Hard containers (concrete, metal) with sharp corners need shielding to protect the horses. Do not site troughs at right angles through a fence line as this forms dangerous projections on which horses can injure themselves. Placing containers in the corner of a paddock can also create injuries if horses hassle each other for space.

starches and sugars

Carbohydrates produce energy and heat, and excess intake is stored as fat for future use. Concentrates such as straight grains, cubes or pellets and coarse mixes (sweet feeds) are mainly carbohydrate.

Right: Spring and summer grass is high in proteins, which are required for growth, development and body maintenance.

CARBOHYDRATES ARE THE STARCHES and sugars in the diet; they produce energy and heat, and excess intake is stored as glycogen and fat. Most grain feeds such as oats, barley and maize (corn) are mainly carbohydrate, as are coarse mixes (sweet feeds) and cubes (nuts, pellets), which are made from them. Grass contains a good deal of sugar in spring and autumn, and

also contains carbohydrates in the form of cellulose, which occurs in hay, haylage and straw, too. Popular additives like molasses and the light syrups used to bind branded feeds are sources of carbohydrate as is sugar beet pulp, which is rich in mainly fibre-based carbohydrate (much of the sugar having been removed during processing for the human food industry) and is an excellent way of giving horses safe energy.

Because of the high sugar content in spring and autumn grass, grazing in these seasons should start with short spells of just half an hour, and maybe limited to about a couple of hours a day. Research indicates that animals prone to laminitis should be turned out when the sugar content of the grass is at its lowest in the 24-hour cycle – between midnight and 2am!

proteins

PROTEINS ARE THE ONLY foods able to make body tissues and they can also provide some heat and energy. Excess can be stored as fat but then loses its tissue-making properties. Some excess protein is excreted by the kidneys which, if it is overdone, can become inflamed and injured. I remember a racehorse trainer who frequently tested his horses' kidneys by applying fingertip pressure to their loins. This was in the days when protein overload was a real risk because large amounts of 'straight' or individual grain feeds were commonly fed, plus beans and peas, which are high in energy and protein. With today's commercial, branded feeds it is much easier to avoid. Because of its importance in maintaining the body and its inability to be stored, a daily supply of protein is important.

Most feeds contain protein and many carbohydrate sources also contain some. Spring grass is rich in it as well as carbohydrates.

If a protein supplement or boost is needed as with a debilitated horse or backward foal, special products could be recommended by a vet or nutritionist. Milk products are now back in favour as research has disproved the theory that adult horses cannot digest milk.

what makes feed?

fats

Most horses much prefer haylage to hay. Haylage is also better for those with respiratory allergies or sensitivities as it is not prone to dust and moulds, which can be found in even the best of hay.

FEEDING HIGH-FAT, high-oil diets to hard-working endurance horses, eventers, hunters and the like is an effective way of providing extra energy, particularly if they are at the limits of their appetites. Too much, though, is felt to coat the gut wall and actually prevent the absorption of nutrients.

A good way to provide extra oil is to give a tablespoon of soya or corn oil mixed in each feed (say twice daily); up to a cupful can be given, on expert advice. Another way is to use a linseed and/or fenugreek (a herb) mixture as an additive.

Most cereal grains contain some fat; barley usually contains more than oats. High-fat diets should also be high in choline and vitamin E to ensure adequate chemical breakdown during digestion; a nutritionist, or a vet interested in nutrition, could advise you on this.

extras or not?

VITAMINS, MINERALS and trace elements are essential in the diet, being necessary for the processing of the other feed constituents and for certain body functions. Many good makes of branded feeds are fully supplemented for normal purposes, but vitamins, minerals and trace elements are also available separately in the expensive and often confusing products displayed and advertised everywhere. It is tempting to rush out and buy them, believing that this will give our horse a new zest for life and enable him to win Badminton or the Golden Horseshoe with no other help, but in practice, indiscriminate feeding of such supplements is not only expensive but also can cause overdosing and imbalances.

Horses can make certain nutrients within their body from their feed and can convert others. This, along with the nutrients their diet already contains, may mean that supplementation is not necessary. It is worth the relatively small fee to get reliable advice from an expert on what nutrients, if any, are likely to be missing from your

horse's diet and whether a broad-spectrum (wide-ranging) product or simply a single, specialized one – maybe even a single vitamin or mineral – should be used. (Nutrition/feed companies often have a free service.)

Owners who still prefer to feed 'straights', such as oats, barley and maize, rather than professionally made and commercially

available mixes can, unwittingly, be providing an unbalanced diet. In these cases, a supplement might well be needed. Again, advice should be sought as most owners, professional or amateur, simply don't have the scientific knowledge or training, or the laboratory facilities, to analyse their own feeds or to understand a lab analysis when it arrives.

forage Good brands of bagged haylage or semi-wilted forage (produced by a different process) will have detailed

analysis panels on the bag, which will help your vet or nutritionist to integrate the product into your horse's diet, and hay and haylage can be analysed to obtain the same information. The best merchants will have had their goods analysed and should be able to give you the details. Farm-produced haylage in Britain, usually delivered in giant or smaller rounded or rectangular bales wrapped in plastic can be 'really good stuff', as one nutritionist put it, but you should still really get an analysis of it, too, if you are doing any serious work with your horse.

In addition, if your horses are fed mainly or only hay or haylage, you may need a supplement to ensure that they are getting all their vitamins and minerals. Such products are simply fed mixed with a little of a short-chopped forage, maybe with grated carrot or apple to ensure that it all goes down.

STORAGE

As with reputable feeds, a 'use by' date should be given on the pack of any good supplement; after this the efficacy of the nutrients it contains may be reduced, so it is obviously wise to use them before. The way you store supplements can have an effect, too. Making sure that the container is firmly closed after use helps it to keep its quality, but it is as well to keep supplements in cool, dark conditions, too. Most supplements are well packed in resealable plastic tubs or bottles or glass containers, the latter much favoured by ecologists and enthusiasts of organic feeds because glass is inert and does not affect the substance inside it which, apparently, some plastics can. (Some experts also advise that we should not feed or water horses from plastic containers.) One hopes that a reputable firm will have checked this out before using plastic to pack their product.

fibre – the essential ingredient

FIBRE IS THE MAIN component that provides the essential bulk in a diet which gives a horse a feeling of being satisfied by his food. Also referred to as roughage, it is the tough, fibrous cell walls of the plant and comes in two main types – cellulose, which is a form of carboyhydrate and can be digested, and lignin, which is woody, indigestible and can be seen as little 'splinters' in a horse's droppings. The purpose of lignin is to physically break up concentrated feed and allow the digestive juices to penetrate, and also to stimulate peristalsis. The gut will not work effectively if there is not enough bulky material passing down it.

Many people do not feed anything like enough fibre. Many horses suffer hours – day and night – of hunger, boredom and physical discomfort (all of which causes stress and can produce psychological and physical problems) because their owners do not understand – or accept – that good fibre is the most important feed horses can have, is not 'fattening' and is far more important than concentrates.

sources and types

FIBRE OCCURS IN straw, hay, haylage, silage (not usually suitable for working horses) and grass, and also forms the outside husk of grains, with oats having the most. Coarse mixes (sweet feeds) contain fibre, but even so-called high-fibre cubes do not contain enough to make up for insufficient hay or haylage. There are also various forage feeds (fibrous feeds) available. They are usually sold short-chopped (see p.118) in plastic sacks and with vitamins, minerals and trace elements added, and sometimes light syrups for palatability. They range from those suitable for hard-working horses to those for resting animals, 'fatties' and laminitics. They can be used fully or partially as hay replacers and you can add sugar beet pulp or other roots and fruits, and also supplements and, if appropriate, concentrates.

Short-chopped forages are chewed more times than the same weight of long fibre such as hay and haylage and so keep horses occupied longer – a major consideration for stabled or yarded horses. Tests on 'environmental enrichment' also show that horses are more content when given several different types of forage (making up their total ration) at once so they can swap about, as they would in nature.

Bagged haylage and semi-wilted forage are the most expensive forms of forage, but are suitable where only one horse needs such feed. Small 'lady' bales of haylage work out more pricey than large bales of farm-produced haylage, but the latter should be considered only on yards of at least four horses so that they can be used up within roughly five days. 'Lady'

bales are more useful where there are fewer animals.

fibre is enough Obviously, it is necessary to make sure that horses are fed according to their individual needs. Provided the grass is of reasonable quality, grass-fed, healthy horses can hack, show and do similar work without any other feeds, with no trouble at all. During the two world wars, as oats and other feeds traditionally used for horses were in very short supply and mainly reserved for feeding the human population, horses that hunted worked hard and thrived on good hay alone in many cases, plus what winter grass they could get.

In the 1970s, an expert horseman and teacher wrote an article describing how he trained point-to-pointers on the best hay with few or no concentrates. Today, many endurance horses are noted for performing their strenuous work on significant amounts of grass plus judicious rations of other feeds, such as hay or haylage, along with forage feeds and some concentrates.

Haylage is suitable for most horses. If you have previously fed hay, and want to change to haylage, as with any new feed, you should introduce it slowly by mixing it at first with the normal hay ration and gradually increasing the proportion until the haylage has replaced all the hay.

Even ponies, cobs and other good doers usually need hay or haylage outside the grass growing season. This will help to keep them warm and prevent kicking matches due to boredom and hunger.

FEEDING NATURALLY

The way to think of feeding is that horses evolved to be fibre-digesters (forages, grass, hay and haylage, straws such as oat and barley): grain is rarely available to wild and feral equines and the improved grains used for domestic horses are obviously quite unnatural to them – horses have not adapted to digest large quantities of cereal grains or the compound feeds based on them, and it is only now that owners, managers and trainers are finally realizing this. That is not to say that concentrates are bad for horses or that they are never needed: the important point is that concentrates should be fed in much smaller amounts than traditionally used and only when really needed. Hard-working horses may need some, as may old horses, particularly old Thoroughbreds, debilitated horses, those living out in winter (as a top-up to high-quality fibre), and so on. Heavies, cobs and ponies could probably do well solely on forage feeds (plus hay or haylage and maybe sugar beet) with a broad-spectrum vitamin and mineral supplement.

all-important – fibre

grass is fibre too

Above: Very poor grazing, such as this, does not make for contented horses. It is better to give it a chance to grow and turn the horses out on a surfaced area with hay or haylage meanwhile.

Opposite: Contrary to popular opinion, horses do eat long grass, and too much of it can cause problems.

THE BEST TYPE of grazing for horses comprises a very wide range of grasses, herbs and other plants as these give the widest range of minerals and, to the horses, that all important variety in taste. As farming has become more intensive, so the number of grass species in pastures has decreased from a fairly natural 50 or so to a highly artifical less than ten. Such grassland is generally aimed at producing high milk yields in dairy herds or plenty of tender meat in beef animals; it stands to reason, therefore, that it is not very suitable for horses as it is far too rich and restricted. Most horses are unlikely to limit their intake voluntarily so their grazing time must be restricted or they must be put on poorer pasture. Apart from the obvious hazards of rich grazing (particularly in spring and autumn), which may cause serious problems such as laminitis, colic and lymphangitis, a huge weight of grass in the intestine is not conducive to strenuous work – a working horse has enough to do to carry or pull us around without being burdened with his own excess bodyweight.

If having a traditional meadow is not a possibility, a grass seed (pasture) mix specially formulated to provide nutrients for athletic working horses will go a long way towards producing suitable grazing and reducing the likelihood of any problems.

Several equine grassland firms now provide such mixes, and mixes for other purposes such as breeding animals, retired horses and so on.

Where a horse is working very hard, he can also be helped to perform well, by being given a more suitable diet, which is where concentrates come in useful. By using some concentrates, we can top him up with the extra fuel he may need, particularly in cold weather, without weighing him down with the fibrous bulk present in large amounts of grass, hay and haylage.

Meadow hay is the term used for hay (and haylage) cut from pastures that resemble old-fashioned pastures and, at least in the UK, is becoming more widely available.

analysis Of course, you cannot tell just how much grass your horse is consuming, so this is one area of feeding where you may have to operate a wait-and-see policy. However, by having your soil analysed and your herbage (grass and other things) assessed, you can find out the nutrient content and estimate the likely effect it will have on your horses. Using such details, a nutritionist could put a suitable diet together for your horse, also taking into account any other fibre you feed, roots and concentrates.

FIBRE PROPORTION

Most good equine nutritionists now advise that, even for the hardest working horses, the fibre portion of the diet should never fall below two thirds by weight of the total ration, making the concentrate portion no more than one third by weight. Roots, for these purposes, are classed as fibre. Generally, a horse's diet should be kept as high in fibre-based carbohydrate and as low in cereal-based carbohydrate as is practicable for his work and genuine needs.

A common objection to grass and roots (see also p.120) is that they are high in water but this does not matter as the horse simply reduces the amount he drinks. Water passes quite quickly through the digestive tract, too, and the excess is expelled in the urine.

all-important – fibre

for fatties and laminitics

HAYLAGE IS GENERALLY higher in nutrients than hay so the horse gets more from his fodder, which may mean he puts on weight or becomes silly. The answer is to resist the temptation to give him too much coarse mix (sweet feed). It is clearly not needed in

Good doers need a low-energy diet with ample fibre and an appropriate vitamin and mineral supplement. Youngsters up to three years old may also require a protein supplement.

such a case! You should buy forage of a lower energy grade (see p.123) and/or feed it from a small-hole haynet, provided your horse is not one of those who cannot be bothered to make the effort and ends up not eating enough. There are also short-chopped forage feeds formulated for such animals, which will allow him to satisfy his hunger as nature intended.

Feeds for 'fatties' may not be ideal for those prone to laminitis as they do contain minimal levels of certain sugars, for palatability, and these may be enough to trigger the disease in those susceptible to it. Forage feeds specially for laminitics are available and should clearly state this.

chop, not chaff

SHORT-CHOPPED FORAGES are often called chaff. The correct term, if you're interested, is chop because they are simply fibre chopped up short, chop being an old-fashioned feed used for many generations to mix with grains to force the horse to chew and eat slowly. Chaff is the outside

husk of grain left after threshing (separating the wheat from the chaff, as it were, or separating grain from husk). Short-chopped forage feeds are prepared like chop and are made from dried grasses and straw but now often have lucerne (alfalfa) added, plus syrups or sugars and vitamins, minerals and trace elements.

Chop and short-chopped forages are ideal for feeding ad lib when good hay and haylage are in short supply. Mixed with soaked sugar beet pulp (ideally the non-molassed shreds as these are higher in bio-available, fibre-based energy than the molassed and ground, pelleted sort), they form a nutritious, balanced and satisfying feed without the need for concentrates. Grated carrots and apples can be added for extra scrumptiousness. A food processor is ideal for grating carrots for only one or two horses. Chops and short-chopped forages can, of course, be simply fed alone and damped to keep horses full and busy.

OCCUPATIONAL THERAPY

Apart from being valuable feeds, because they need to be really chewed well, hay and haylage keep animals occupied during long, idle hours – a horse's equivalent of reading a book or watching television. They can give many hours of contented munching, after which the horse may stand and doze or lie down to rest, so a constant supply of fibre is an invaluable aid to working horse owners. Short-chopped forages take even longer to chew and a couple of containers kept filled with the different sorts would also help keep him interested, not to mention satisfied.

buy it right

Stabling horses for most of their time is not good horsemastership. They become sad, frustrated and bored as, indeed, these appear to be.

IT IS CHEAPER to buy fibrous feeds, such as hay and haylage or feeding straws, such as oat or barley, off the field – while it is still growing. This is ideal if you have storage facilities for many bales, but you must stipulate that the purchase depends on the resulting quality being good. Buying at harvest time, or at least as early in the autumn as you can, is also a good plan. The price will invariably go up as winter

MOULD OR YEAST

Modern haylages are drier than the sort previously available but should still be freer of dust than hay is. Haylage is particularly good for horses with respiratory problems who are allergic to the spores often found on apparently 'clean' samples of hay and which often triggers the allergic condition known colloquially as 'broken wind' or 'heaves'.

Although mould on hay is often white, it is also dry and dusty. Do not confuse this with the white yeasts that sometimes form on baled, moist, wrapped haylage. The yeasts are, I am assured, harmless. You can always take a small sample to your vet to see if he or she thinks it worth having analysed.

passes and you could be paying double the autumn price by spring, and certainly by early summer. In fact, it could work out cheaper to pay rent on storage space and buy a big load (although properly wrapped haylage can be kept outdoors, of course) than to suffer high fodder prices in the early part of the new year. Make sure you have a clear, written agreement that any 'bad' bales can be returned for exchange or credit.

Although many owners are tempted to operate a wait-and-see policy, in practice it really pays to think ahead, pinpoint local supplies in the field and secure your requirements for the coming months or year at harvest time. If you have trouble doing this, it's worth contacting your merchant or the maker direct and asking about bulk purchase discount possibilities, maybe getting together with other owners, which should ensure the best price, too. How is it that the marketers of short-chopped forages can get supplies when we ordinary mortals can't? The answer is that they not only usually have their own suppliers (or land for crops) in their own region, but also have contacts around the country and abroad, to ensure that their businesses keep running and supplies are always available. No matter how bad a hay or haylage crop has been, these firms always seem to be able to come up with the goodies for our horses.

feed and exercise

before or after?

Opposite: Provided you walk your horse for his first 20 minutes, there is no reason why you should not exercise him shortly after feeding. Fast work, like this, though, should not be carried out within the hour.

WE HAVE ALL HAD it drummed into us that it is bad to work a horse immediately after a feed because of the digestive and respiratory problems that this can cause. The stomach and lungs lie right next to one another, separated only by a thin, but strong sheet of muscle, called the diaphragm, between the chest cavity (which contains the heart and lungs) and the abdomen (which contains the stomach, intestines and other organs). During work, the lungs have to expand and the heart has to work more than during rest. A full stomach next to them will interfere with their action, and the blood supply will be diverted from digestion to supply energy to the muscles, so the stomach's workings are also affected.

However, those horses that have constant supplies of fibrous feeds rarely gorge themselves in the way that those left for many hours without feed do, so working the former sensibly is not a problem. Wild and feral equines eat almost constantly and often have to take to their heels full tilt to escape predators: if nature had not equipped them with an escape mechanism, they could constantly be going down with colic and twisted gut, and the species would quickly die out.

Therefore: exercising straight after a moderate feed is fine, provided that the work is slow, mainly walk, a steady trot introduced after about 20 minutes. Fast work is another matter.

If you give your horse so much fibre that he will have only finished it an hour or two before morning work, you should avoid problems. If he finishes at, say, 5am, you can take him out in the early morning before his breakfast, safe in the knowledge that he is not particularly hungry, and that you are not working him straight after a feed. You can work out how much hay you need to feed to ensure this situation by first leaving so much that he still has some left in the morning. Weigh the leavings and deduct that amount from the total amount you left him the night before. For his next night's ration, take the resulting figure (the amount he actually ate) and leave him about 2kg (4–5lb) less than that.

In the morning, exercise your horse first then give him some hay while you put away tack and so on. Then give him his bucket feed, if he has one, and leave him with two large bins or nets of hay or haylage and forage feed while you go off to earn the money to buy him some more. Or you could give him his bucket feed on return, stock up his shelter with hay unless he's getting good grass, then turn him into his paddock or yard.

ROOTS – SAFE AS TREATS OR PART OF THE MAIN COURSE

Carrots have received a poor press recently because of their supposed high sugar content, which some people believe causes behavioural problems in their horses. In fact, roots generally consist of around 90 per cent water and the rest is mainly fibre. The sugar content in carrots is so low that a horse would have to eat more of them than he could probably manage for it to have an effect on his behaviour. They are a valuable winter succulent and about 2kg (4lb) of carrots a day should be fine for a 225kg (500lb) horse.

Soaked sugar beet pulp contains some sugar but is mainly water and fibre; again, it is a valuable winter succulent. The unmolassed, shredded variety seems to be favoured by nutritionists as it provides fibre-based energy on a slow-release basis.

how much to feed

condition scoring

CONDITION SCORING is a way of assessing your horse's bodyweight or condition by his appearance. It is important to be able to judge accurately whether your horse is too thin, too fat or just right. The areas of the horse used for the assessment are the top of the neck, the back and ribs and the hindquarters over the croup and down the buttocks. Scores range from 0 to 5.

0 is emaciated – virtually skin and bone
Poor ewe neck with a narrow base, backbone sharp and protruding, ribs easily seen, croup and hipbones (wings of pelvis) protruding, hollow flanks, no flesh between buttocks.

1 is poor
Minor improvement on 0, poor neck with a narrow base, ribs easily seen, backbone easily discerned and bony to the touch, croup and hip bones obvious, hollow under tail.

2 is moderate/fair
Straight neck with no topline, narrow at base but with a little tone, ribs can be seen and easily felt, backbone just covered but vertebrae easy to feel, croup easily felt, quarter muscles flat (little development), hip bones easily felt, buttock muscles poor.

3 is good/normal
Neck showing some topline (given good conformation), firm muscle tone, vertebral spinous processes defined but not prominent, back well-covered in muscle, ribs cannot be seen but can be easily felt, quarters covered but hip bones can be felt, more flesh under tail.

4 is fat
Neck showing some crest and starting to become hardened with ridges of fat forming, ribs cannot be seen and are hard to feel, maybe gutter between fat along the backbone, hips hard to feel.

5 is obese
Hard, marked crest with wrinkles of fat, notable gutter down spine to root of tail, ribs, croup and hipbones barely felt, if at all, excessively rounded quarters.

Clearly, we should all be aiming at achieving as close to score 3 as we can. Many people who have good doers use this as an excuse for their overweight state and others say that they don't like their animals too fat as it puts too much stress on them. Neither of these are excuses for having horses too fat or too thin. Regulation of the diet and appropriate work will correct matters unless there are other, clinical reasons for the problem.

Checkpoints for condition scoring

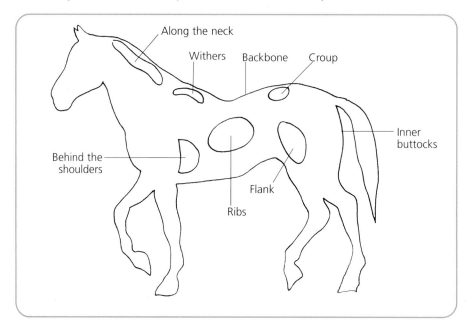

Along the neck · Withers · Backbone · Croup · Inner buttocks · Behind the shoulders · Flank · Ribs

weight plus work

This horse, a Shire cross, is probably a very good doer and, for general purposes, will need a low-energy diet.

A weightape will give a good enough idea of how much to feed your horse. This tape is being used a little too far forward and is on the withers; its reading will be giving a false impression that the horse is heavier than he is.

THE SIMPLEST METHOD of calculating how much to feed a horse or pony is to use his bodyweight and workload. The most accurate way of finding out how much he weighs is to weigh him, with only his bridle on, at your nearest weigh bridge. If this is inconvenient, you can buy one of the special tapes designed for the purpose from tack stores, feed companies and some veterinary practices. Experts say these are not really accurate enough but, in practice, they'll do fine – each animal varies according to the efficiency of his metabolism anyway, and you can adjust the feed as you go along.

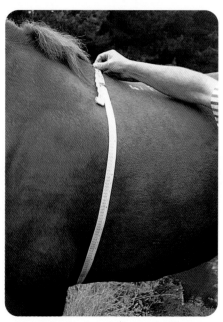

The tapes are graduated so that you read off the horse's measurement around the girth, his weight and consequent daily food requirement. Clearly, this will need modifying according to his work regime. Place the tape around the girth, just behind the withers, making sure it is straight (vertical) and not twisted, and that you take the measurement at the end of one of the horse's out breaths so that it just presses in the skin.

A cob, pony or good doer should have about 2 per cent of his bodyweight daily in total weight of feed, maybe less, especially if he is overweight and/or not working. For

other horses that are resting or in light work, it should be 2.5 per cent. For medium work (see pp.29–33), give 2.5 per cent but maybe use higher-energy feeds. For hard work, give 3 per cent of bodyweight, and possibly give higher energy feeds and/or extra oil.

feed energy levels

Along with the nutritional analysis of the contents, all good quality feed bags also list the amount of energy their contents supply in megajoules (MJ) of digestible energy (DE) per kilogram (kg). The energy supplied by hay and haylage depends on the type of grasses they contain and the production methods.

For resting horses or those in light work give probably all the ration as good quality fibre. If you need to top up on the fibre, concentrated feeds of an energy level of about 8.5MJ of DE/kg are suitable. Ponies, cobs and good doers need a lower level than this.

For medium work, an energy level of about 10MJ of DE/kg can be used, say mainly high-nutrient fibre feeds with perhaps up to a quarter of the ration by weight as concentrates, if necessary.

For hard work, an energy level of about 13MJ of DE/kg can be used, with no less than two thirds of the ration as fibre and the rest concentrates, if necessary. Extra oil can provide energy without more concentrates.

grassland management

care of a valuable asset

GRASS IS ONE of the cheapest and, of course, most natural feeds you can give your horse. During spring, summer and autumn, it provides a valuable and much appreciated element in his diet. Indeed, if he is living out, resting or in light to even moderate work, and the grass is suitable, not too rich or too poor, he could well need no other feed.

To be productive, land and grass needs care. The field must be well-drained as wet land is cold and oxygen-starved producing poor grass growth, and it normally seethes with flies in summer. Weeds and poisonous plants should be removed, not least to give room for decent grass to grow.

Land that is neglected and overused, deteriorates until it is useless for anything but exercise. Land without a good covering of grass has no protection from horses' hooves, which further damages the grass roots, compounding the problem.

Soil type varies widely, even from field to field in some localities so it is worth having it assessed by an expert. In the UK, the Equine Services Department of DEFRA offers an excellent advisory service on equine grassland management – and should also be able to tell you about eco-

friendly ways of getting rid of weeds – and so do some grass seed companies. In the USA, contact your County Extension Agent. If you are planning to reseed, stress that your land is for horses, not other species, so that you get a suitable grass mix. Nitrogen-rich plant species (and fertilizers) are not good for horses and can cause digestive and circulatory problems. Help the seed supplier by describing the way you manage your horses and ponies. Ask for as many suitable species as possible in your mix and also arrange to have a herb strip sown on the driest, sunniest part of your land so that the horses have variety and can use their instinct to eat what they need. Don't mix the herb seeds in with the grasses as they will be smothered.

paddock rotation When the vegetation is sorted out, you'll need a rotation scheme to keep the land in good condition. Try to divide your land into at least two parts, preferably three, so that each can be used, treated and rested in

Chain harrowing is an excellent way to aerate the land and tear out dead vegetation, which allows light to reach new grass.

turn. After horses have grazed the land for three or four weeks, move them to the next area, cut the long grass they have left and harrow the field to aerate it and pull out dead grass and roots. Apply any recommended fertilizer (ideally organic and not pig slurry or poultry manure as these produce over-rich grazing for horses) then rest the treated land. Continue grazing around it like this.

If you are responsible for a good spread of land, you'll have to buy a harrow and a gang mower or get someone else to do it in return for payment or in exchange for services from you. Small areas can be dealt with manually, although it's hard work. Become handy with a scythe or sickle and train your horses to pull a harrow! If you do not have your own land, at least your knowledge of this simple basic care plan will help you recognize whether your livery stables are doing a proper job or not.

companion grazing In the wild, of course, different species of animal graze together. In domesticity, horses and cattle make complementary grazing

partners, and some people are all in favour of sheep. The point is that different animals eat different grasses and parts of grasses.

In paddocks horses form lavatory areas where they do not graze. The droppings build up, the grass grows long and unpalatable and the horses ignore it, favouring instead 'lawn' areas, which they keep clean and crop down. Cattle cannot cope with short grass: they eat the long grass that the horses have wasted and drop their manure on the nutrient-depleted lawn areas. Where horses' droppings are not regularly picked up, worm eggs and larvae (see p.126) infest the lavatory areas, and the cattle take these in, killing the parasites. When spread on the horse's lavatory areas after mowing, cattle manure can disguise the smell of horse droppings, which horses dislike, and cause them to graze there again. This is surely a domestic version of what happens in the wild.

Sheep can and do eat right down to the ground but, in my experience, do not deal with long grass. Their droppings do not seem to benefit the land as much as cattle muck, but they are better than nothing.

You don't have to graze different animals together at the same time, but try to get some visitors on your land at some point during spring, summer or autumn. Give llamas a try.

SAFETY NOTES

If you graze cattle with your horses, go for the hornless kind to avoid the chance of nasty injuries.

When using either cattle or sheep as complementary grazing partners and to help break the lifecycle of equine parasites, take veterinary advice. Some products that are routinely fed to cattle, such as hormones, drugs and antibiotics, and the organophosphates with which sheep are dipped, can cause environmental and health problems.

worms and worming

controls

PICKING UP HORSE DROPPINGS from your land is the very best way to keep the land and your horses as parasite-free as is practically possible. Attitudes to worm control are changing as research goes on, but the feeling now is largely that horses should be tested for worm burdens by means of faecal counts and possibly blood tests for alien proteins, and only those showing an infestation of more than 50 eggs per gram of faeces need to be treated.

'Poo-picking' may be an unpopular job but done daily or every other day, it does not build up to monumental proportions, as here. This field must be a real hot bed of parasite infestation.

If you pick up droppings every two or, at most, three days during the grass-growing season, and even during a mild winter, your horses will eventually become and remain parasite-free, for all practical purposes. Scattering droppings merely increases the contaminated area.

The smaller your area of land and the more equines you have on it, the more rigorous you need to be about worm checks, droppings removal and land care. Larger areas permit a more relaxed attitude, but it is still important to have your horses checked on a regular basis and to treat them accordingly.

Remember that it is not only horses at grass that need worming: animals in stables can pick up worms from the floor or walls if they lick them or eat from the ground, and worm lifecycles can take anything from weeks to months to complete. Warm, moist weather is the most conducive to worm production. Hot, dry weather and hard frosts desiccate or kill larvae and eggs.

Opinions change on the best way to rid your horse of parasites. It is vital to keep up to date on this important topic by checking with your veterinary practice, and reading the equestrian press.

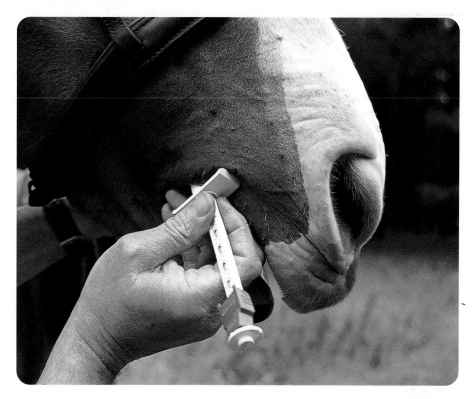

remedies

ANTHELMINTICS (WORMING MEDICINES) are highly toxic and to put these poisons through your horse every few weeks or months cannot be ideal for their health – or your pocket as they are not cheap. More effective drugs are constantly being developed to kill more parasites and at more stages of their development than ever before and at longer intervals, and they are an improvement on their predecessors. The main conventional worming drugs currently belong to four chemical groups – benzimidazole, ivermectin, pyrantel and moxidectin, sold under various trade names. These kill different equine parasites around the world, however, there is still no catch-all drug that kills all internal parasites at all stages of development.

Holistic therapies are coming more and more into their own after a 50-year domination by the 'heavy gang' (as one herbalist put it). They all have their place and my own experience has shown that homoeopathic remedies can be very effective for internal parasite control. Herbal remedies, too, help greatly, garlic being one traditional favourite for horses and dogs. Grazing with cattle (p.125), helps greatly to break the lifecycle of equine parasites. If you prefer to use drugs, consult your veterinary practice on the latest thinking and wormers that are available, and follow their advice. If you want to reduce the amount of wormer you use, why not go for complementary therapies plus carrying out regular faecal worm counts or blood tests through your veterinary practice, only using drugs for selected horses, if indicated?

Your vet should discuss a suitable worming regime with you before selling you a product. He or she will need to know about your horse's type, state of health and his lifestyle and environment, and will then be able to help you formulate the best year-round de-worming programme.

WHY WORM?

Most adult worms of most species congregate in the horse's gut where they cause damage to the bowel wall, which can result in bouts of colic. Larvae can damage tissues as they migrate around the body, and potentially fatal aneurysms (ballooned arteries) are common in bad infestations. Worms also cause blockages and unthriftiness, as well as death.

grooming

GROOMING IS a time-consuming task and one which can be quite hard work for the inexperienced and unfit. It is certainly necessary, though, because it aids your horse's health and condition and it enables you to monitor the state of his skin and coat, if you do it thoroughly. It is no

Turning your horses out rugged up (keep the rugs as lightweight as possible) will help to minimize the amount of time spent grooming especially in winter when daylight hours are precious.

pleasure to ride or drive a dirty horse; it is also bad for public relations to be seen out scruffy and unkempt with a dirty, equally unkempt horse.

Skin has a limited lifespan and sheds dead scales from its outer layer throughout the year; these scales are the dandruff seen in an ungroomed horse's coat. Skin also produces natural oils to lubricate itself and the coat hairs to give some protection against wet weather and cold. The main times of casting the old coat and growing a new one are spring and autumn, and when this occurs is mainly dependent on the number of hours of light, natural or otherwise, the horse experiences. The light passing through the horse's eye is noted by the brain which controls the hormones governing the shedding and growing process.

grooming – briefly

Grooming starts with dandy brushing or rubbing with a rough cloth or piece of sacking to remove mud, dried sweat, muck and dead hair. Dandy brushes have long, stiff bristles and should be used considerately. Horses carrying a lot of dried mud may be done with rubber or plastic curry combs.

Body brushing comes next: the body brush has short, fine and dense bristles to penetrate to the skin (impossible in a normal winter coat). It should be held with a stiff arm and slightly bent elbow. Lean your weight on the arm to push the bristles through the coat, rather than pushing with your arm and shoulder; this is less tiring and just as effective (see p.75 for some ideas on saving grooming time).

MUD PLUS MORE MUD

Dealing with mud can be a big problem for working horse owners on limited time. A lightweight waterproof sheet or normal turnout rug will keep him dry, according to the weather, and save you a lot of time and effort. Just make sure mud is cleaned off the girth area and the head as best you can, so you do not encourage rubbing and galls.

wet worries If your horse is damp but clean (perhaps after you've hosed him off), it's fine to tack up and get on and exercise. There's very little difference between this kind of wet and the sweat that a horse produces under tack anyway. An absorbent or permeable numnah between the horse and his saddle (and a girth) may make him more comfortable, perhaps also a cotton webbing bridle. I have done this countless times and had no trouble.

clipping

CLIP AS LITTLE AS POSSIBLE for your horse's comfort, to save time and effort managing rugs and to save on feed bills. Rugs do not fully make up for the loss of the natural coat.

For a horse in light work and a working owner who is doing their horse themself, there is no doubt that it saves time, effort and money not to clip and there is usually no need to do so. The horse will be more comfortable with his natural coat, unless it is very thick or greasy and he sweats up even with light work. If he is not working at all there is no point in clipping, even if he spends some time stabled in the winter. A horse kept on the combined system (p.10), say, and doing light work but with a fine coat should not need clipping, either.

I feel that it is unkind to hunter clip or clip out fine-skinned horses; if you must clip, even thick-coated horses doing fast work in winter will feel better with at least a good patch left on their back, loins and quarters and maybe the upper neck, particularly if they are hunters and so kept hanging around a good deal between spells of possibly fast work. A blanket clip is an excellent clip for even very hard working horses and, going down the scale, there is the chaser clip, the trace clip and the Irish clip, ending with what can be called a bib clip (just the chest and underneath the neck clipped off) for children's ponies, cobs and lightly working horses or ponies.

Save time, effort and money, by not overdoing the clipping. Your horse will be much more comfortable in his natural coat, especially if he is having an easy winter, with plenty of turn out time.

and others believe that the hair is there for protection. This protection doesn't always work in my experience.

tops and tails I dislike trimmed docks and much prefer the tops of tails to be full or plaited (braided); this way the horse can have the necessary protection of his full tail when needed. The 'antennae' whiskers around the horse's muzzle and eyes should be left on as they are not simply untidy hairs but part of the horse's sensory system – you wouldn't remove a cat's whiskers would you? Likewise, the hair inside the ears should be left to prevent dirt, debris and insects getting down into them and causing real problems and discomfort. The edges and bases of the ears, however, can be neatened up with scissors. The under-jaw hairs can be snipped off with scissors and a comb. One thing is for sure: trimming these areas with clippers gives the horse a shaved, amateurish look so get skilled with scissors and comb!

trimming

COMPETENT TRIMMING can make a tremendous difference to the appearance of even an unclipped horse and puts the finishing touches to a clipped one. Overtrimming, though, makes any horse look deprived and not quite right.

The main areas to trim for neatness and ease of management are the forelock, mane, under the jaw, the edges of the ears and the heels. The latter is the subject of differences of opinion as some say that mud fever is easier to avoid and treat if the hair is removed (the latter is certainly true)

no hoof, no horse

THE UNDERSIDE OF the feet, like the teeth, often come into the 'out-of-sight-out-of-mind' category, yet the feet, their condition and their balance are crucial to a comfortable, non-stressed, agile and competent athlete. They should be picked out and the shoes checked before and after every ride – on average twice a day and more if they are getting packed with manure, snow, mud or other debris. As most owners know, you spend more money on your farrier than your vet in normal circumstances. Horses in even moderate work usually need a new set of shoes about every six weeks and even those in light work will need the shoes removing, the feet trimming and the same ones replacing.

If your horse is not working for a season, have his shoes removed to give his feet a chance to spread naturally and improve the blood circulation through them. They will still need trimming every six weeks or so.

going barefoot

LEAVING YOUR HORSE unshod will save money but not effort or time; however, many horses that are currently shod could well benefit from being unshod. Horses vary greatly in the constitution of their hoof horn, and horses best suited to going unshod (provided he is working on soft or smooth, not too abrasive hard surfaces) have naturally tough, resilient hooves and a good frog, although some breeds, notably the Caspian and some Arabs, have small frogs, evolved in a desert environment, and manage very well.

If you want to try going unshod, discuss things with your farrier. Remember that the correct nutrients for optimal horn quality and production must be present in the diet and that it will take at least six months for the tougher horn to grow down to the ground. Check that his diet is suitable, and give time for the hoof to grow better horn if the existing horn is not tough enough to withstand going unshod. There are various paint-on products aimed at toughening horn but not all are beneficial. It is as well to discuss them with your farrier or vet. Some are excellent and could be a big help. Ordinary hoof oil is partly a waste of money and, if applied to excess, can actually weaken horn by interfering with its natural 'breathing' process.

When the time comes to leave off the shoes, plan a period on soft ground, leave on a little more horn than normal, round off the edges of the feet well to minimize splits and chips, and work for short spells. Gradually bring in smooth, harder going and take it from there. Check the feet carefully when you pick them out (twice a day) and watch your horse's behaviour carefully, too. Be ready to spot him becoming footsore.

Many people feel that they will just have the hind shoes removed and leave on the front ones – to save money. This idea is the product of not thinking things through. Horses are 'rear-wheel drive' animals: they push themselves along from the back, not haul themselves along from the front – unless they have significant physical problems. If we school them correctly, we want them to take more weight on the hindquarters, which can only be transferred to the ground via the hind feet. This puts the hind feet under more stress, so the horse needs more protection, not less, if it is to be comfortable and able to work well.

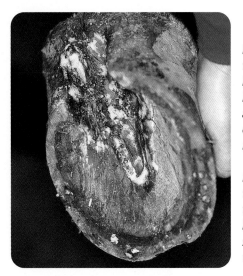

THRUSH

Even between regular six-weekly shoeings, sometimes flaps of horn from the frog grow over the grooves at the sides of the frog or over the cleft, areas that hold moisture and dirt and can favour the development of the diseases of the horn commonly known as thrush. Characterized by a dark discharge and/or an appalling smell, thrush can be very stubborn to clear and if it gets into the deeper horn, it can soon spread to the sensitive tissues. The horse might be more or less lame and some more sensitive ones will resist treatment.

It is a good idea for a sensible owner to keep on hand a sharp knife to be able to trim flaps of excess horn. Dirty and even just wet conditions can also favour the development of thrush and because of its stubborn nature, you should begin treatment at once. This usually involves scrubbing the area daily with saline solution to clean it and applying an effective disinfectant, obtainable from your vet or farrier.

choosing and using rugs

rugs – good or bad?

HORSE CLOTHING – rugs and blankets – is a double-edged sword. Rugs most certainly add a good deal to a horse's comfort, health and cleanliness if they are used only when necessary, only in the amounts necessary, fit properly and are kept decently clean. On the downside is the fact that dealing with rugs creates significant extra work – putting them on, taking them off and maintaining them all takes time – particularly in winter when working owners are invariably busy due to the short days.

Before the onset of winter, rugging heavily, like this, is not necessary. As this appears to be a pony, it is extremely unlikely to need rugging up at all and would be much more comfortable without.

Even in summer, some clothing may be beneficial, such as coolers, anti-sweat rugs, mesh sweet-itch rugs or those that defy insects' attempts to make our horses' lives hell, lightweight turnout sheets for the odd cold summer day (not so odd in the UK and Ireland) and maybe stable sheets to keep dust and flies off the performance horse's groomed coat.

cruel trend
A major disadvantage, from a horse's viewpoint, is the current trend (at least in the UK) among some owners to grossly over-rug their horses. In winter, horses and ponies, clipped or not, are often muffled up in a winter-weight rug over one or two old bed

duvets when they clearly don't need them. In spring, amazingly, some owners cling to this winter habit and still put on at least two rugs and/or a duvet.

I have seen horses with sweat dripping off their bellies and running down their faces, clearly extremely uncomfortable – to the extent that you could wring out the bottom rug. It has been suggested by a health professional that a horse abused like this would probably 'have a splitting headache and be hyperthermic' (with a raised body temperature). Even on warm or hot days, some owners seem quite incapable of leaving their poor, distressed animals without rugs, when it should be obvious to any sensible caring person that they would be far more comfortable without.

This cruel practice can be seen in all sorts of yards from those of 'happy hackers' to those of top competition riders. The excuses given are quite strange, the most common given to me being: 'he feels the cold', 'it keeps him clean', 'he likes being rugged up', 'it keeps his coat flat', 'he needs a summer coat for showing' (it's daylight which will produce that) and – the most stupid of all – 'that's what rugs are for'.

CHILLY CHECK

Check if a horse is cold by placing the flat of your hand around the base of his ears, on his belly, flanks, loins and quarters, giving time for any heat to come through. If there isn't any, he's cold and could do with a rug. If he's warm, he certainly doesn't. In summer, if a mesh rug is needed for protection from insects, fair enough – this is good horse care. If a light sheet is needed to keep a show horse clean just before showing, not all the time, use the lightest one you can for his comfort.

horses for courses

Permeable, synthetic rugs like this are useful for warding off chills after work on cool days if the horse is hot, or when a horse is kept standing around. They are light and easy to handle and launder.

THERE IS A WIDE RANGE of rugs available for various circumstances:

Indoor rugs protect stabled horses against dust and maybe insects and keep clipped or sensitive horses warm in winter. They do not need to be wind- and waterproof; such rugs are an unhealthy option for indoor horses (those stabled or in a covered yard). Indoor rugs should be of a natural or breatheable, permeable fabric so that the horse's natural sweat, which is produced even though we do not notice it, can evaporate away – another good reason for not overloading the horse. In summer, a very lightweight permeable fabric, synthetic or natural (cotton or, if you can find it, linen) is enough, if really necessary.

Outdoor rugs protect horses from the weather and summer ones from insects, too. Outdoor turnout/New Zealand rugs are minor miracles of design and textile technology these days. Mostly synthetic, the fabrics are highly tear-resistant, or even claim to be tear-proof, and should be wind- and waterproof, too. Their linings should definitely be permeable and comfortable to

the horse. Their filling or padding material is warm and lightweight, often with a tog rating, like a duvet for winter or autumn/spring. Some of the light summer ones have an in-built insect-repellent quality in the fabric or even an SPF factor to protect the horse against the sun. The mesh rugs that specifically protect against midges are a life-saver to horses prone to sweet-itch.

Exercise or quarter sheets which fit over the back, loins and quarters under the saddle or over a driving harness help prevent sensitive, working or clipped horses becoming chilled in winter, and can be waterproof or not.

Coolers fasten to the browband and cover the horse from ears to tail; they are for cooling down/drying off after work or washing.

Therapeutic and remedial rugs such as magnetic therapy and physiotherapy rugs are usually the same shape as a stable rug, but are made of special materials or have inserts.

laundering

You really need two turnout rugs so you can keep at least one available, dry and brushed or vacuumed clean. Here, the rug on the horse in the foreground is too tight around the neck and is pulling on the withers and the points of the shoulders because of its poor design.

TURNOUT RUGS GET DIRTY with mud and wet in a very few hours, so it's as well to look for ones you can wash and dry at home, if at all possible. This is where synthetic fabrics come into their own: they're so easy to launder. Some are light enough to put in a domestic washing machine (get them as hair-free as possible first) and even in a tumble drier. It is important to check with the manufacturer just how they should be dealt with as if you ruin them due to careless washing you will be unlikely to receive compensation from the makers.

Natural fabrics such as wool (can often be given a cool wash in the washing machine but don't tumble dry) and cotton (hand-hot machine wash and tumble dry) are a bit more trouble, and really thick rugs will need sending out. Specialist equine laundries and dry cleaners are widely available and often do repairs, too, but it is better if some of your rugs are washable at home as it is inconvenient and expensive to have to keep sending them away. If you do send things to the laundry, pin a note to them to follow the maker's laundering/cleaning instructions to the letter so that they can't say you didn't tell them.

Turnout rugs, in particular, should be bought in pairs so you always have a dry one to use. Far too many people keep horses standing in filthy rugs for weeks or even months and think that this is an acceptable standard.

NATURAL OR SYNTHETIC?

Rug and blanket fabric is becoming more and more technical. From a practical viewpoint, though, you just need to know which qualities you require. Waterproof rugs and those that are waterproof with permeability are usually synthetic although there are still turnout/New Zealand rugs made out of waterproofed cotton canvas. Non-waterproof and permeable rugs are made of natural fabrics or synthetics.

Some rugs with heat-retaining qualities must not be used under heater lamps as otherwise horses can over-heat and even burn.

comfort and fit checklist

MODERN RUGS generally fit much better than those of just five years ago. Spine seams are often not needed now as the use and design of forehand and hindquarter darts to create shape is better understood. Many rugs, though, are still too tight in the forehand and particularly the shoulder. The points of good fit are:

1 Rugs should come in front of the withers, not on top of or behind them.

2 When the front fastening is done up, the neckline should fit up around the base of the neck, not fall down on to the shoulders.

3 You should be able to pass your hand comfortably around the neckline and there should be no pull on the points of the shoulders.

4 The horse must be able to get his head down comfortably to eat at ground level without the rug pulling down on the withers or half choking him.

5 Rugs should extend back to the root of the tail, not finish part way up the horse's hindquarters. Turnout rugs should extend about 15cm (6in) past the root of the tail.

6 Rugs should be deep enough to cover the elbow and stifle on their bottom edge: turnout rugs can be a little longer than this.

7 Insist on the best quality straps/surcingles, having them changed, if necessary. Buckles and clips, particularly, let their rugs down in that they break easily, are difficult to manipulate or, if metal, go rusty.

8 Rubbed hair, bald patches, swelling and raw skin can all be produced by a badly fitting rug.

in the stable

what sort of bed?

APART FROM GIVING your horse somewhere comfortable to lie down, good bedding in a stable or shelter helps keep him warm and so reduces feed costs. It also protects him from bruising on hard floors. Many horses, also, will hold their urine for hours rather than stale on a hard bare floor. It is bad horse management to leave them like this (see box, right).

Deep litter is the most labour- and money-saving way of bedding down horses but is now generally advised against by equine scientists and vets. If you do go for it, you definitely need a very well ventilated (not draughty) stable. The secret of success with deep litter is to be meticulous about removing droppings, otherwise the bed soon turns into an indoor muck heap. This is not easy for owners who work all day and have no horse help. Semi-deep litter is the compromise method used by very many working owners. The bed is deep littered during the week (with droppings and the worst of the wet dug out) and fully mucked out at the weekend. Full mucking out is without argument the healthiest way of bedding down.

mucking out

THE QUICKEST WAYS to deal with straw and shavings respectively are as follows:

straw   First take out all obvious droppings with a shovel, have a quick stamp or poke around for any piles that are covered up, then use a 4-tined fork to pile all the clean bedding in the cleanest corner. Separate all the half-clean straw into another corner so that you are left with the worst stuff. Shovel this out into a large wheelbarrow and give the floor a good sweep. If there's time, wash the floor with a modern, eco-friendly and horse-friendly disinfectant and rinse it well. If you're rushed, leave this or just rinse down, ideally leaving the floor to dry while the horse is out.

To bed down, lay semi-clean material on the floor, bring in the banks (the old, clean stuff) and lay that as a second layer,

then add new straw on top and up around the sides. This way, old banks, which harbour dirt, moulds and bacteria, do not form.

shavings   Remove all obvious piles of droppings with a special multi-tined shavings fork. Knowing your horse's habits, go for the wettest areas and shovel them out. Scrape the cleanest shavings into the cleanest corner and the semi-dirty or damp ones into another, leaving the floor clear to sweep and rinse as for straw.

To bed down, spread the semi-dirty shavings on the floor, lay a layer of the salvaged clean stuff plus the banks, which should not be allowed to build up, then put new shavings around the sides.

Most people do not manage shavings this way as it does take time and effort. A fair compromise is to remove the droppings and wettest areas, filter quickly through the bedding for whatever other bits of droppings you come across (this can take all day if you let it), fill in with the existing banks and put the new shavings around the sides, maybe with some on top. A fuller job can wait till the weekend.

It is important to have your horse's bed down whenever he is in his stable so that he can stale and also lie down to rest in comfort.

THE POINT IS…

Whatever bedding system or material you prefer, the object should always be to keep it as clean and dry as possible. Some say that a damp bed is better for the horse's feet as the moisture helps keep the horn in good condition. It is true that brittle hooves are probably more in need of moisture than oil but, unfortunately, the moisture in a horse's bed is not water, it is urine, which can have a bad effect on hoof horn. Standing a horse in dirty, wet bedding is, of course, the quickest way to give him rotten horn and thrush, plus irritating his respiratory system and causing disease. The horse would not want to lie in his own urine if he had a choice, so this is another reason to keep a dry bed.

I hate the system of leaving horses entirely without bedding during the day or, horror of horrors, all the time. It is considerate to the horse to give him an inviting surface to urinate on so that he doesn't have to hold his urine for hours or contort himself to reach the banks (if there are any). It is also good management to encourage him to lie down as much as possible, especially if he works. Most horses will not lie on an ordinary floor and those who lie on rubber matting end up with large wet (urine) patches down to the skin and bad manure stains – not the way at all to encourage skin health.

exercise and fitness

top task

Exercise is just as good for horses as for us, probably more so as horses evolved to be on the move most of the time. Exercise stimulates all the internal systems – speeding up the metabolism – strengthens the body and satisfies the mind.

EXERCISING IS THE SINGLE most time-consuming task in the working owner's schedule and also one of the most important if the horse is to be kept healthy, let alone fit – a definite A-list job (see p.68). For developing hard, physical fitness, there is no getting out of ridden or driven work, although to some extent, you can also use loose schooling, such as jumping, groundwork or lungeing or, preferably, long-reining.

The worst months for giving your horse enough exercise are those with the shortest days, December and January in the northern hemisphere and June and July in the southern hemisphere, with the months on either side of them also being difficult. The shortest day of the year is 21st

December or 21st June respectively, so after that you can console yourself that it is all downhill to spring, with lighter nights if not yet milder weather.

The amount of exercise a horse has should depend more on his needs than on his owner's inclinations or time availability, although it is often difficult to reconcile the two. An hour a day, though, is barely enough to keep a horse ticking over, but combined with turning out it may be adequate. Provided horses are used to being turned out, they can still be turned out on frozen fields as they will not go crazy with excitement at the unaccustomed liberty. They also come in clean and dry! Working owners who have no access to turn out facilities should, somehow, aim to get their horses exercised for two hours a day, maybe with help from someone else. On restricted exercise, even in winter, it may be best to omit concentrate feeds, but don't skimp on the fibre (see pp.114–119).

Most exercise is done at the walk, but steady trotting and canters will have to be arranged if fitness is your aim. Some people disapprove of trotting on roads but, at nothing faster than a working trot, it's OK. If you turn out a concentrate-fed horse in winter, you may find that his time in the field keeps him half fit, particularly if he has company, as horses keep each other on the move. Then, more of your ride can be spent at a steady trot, lessening the total amount of time you need to spend on exercising.

In the cold, black mornings of winter, it is so tempting not to tear yourself out of bed in the middle of the night to exercise your horse, and if you are only going to work moderately at weekends, it may not be necessary, provided he can be turned out somewhere. But if you want a fairly fit horse, you will certainly have to ride on two and preferably three other days of the week, if only to keep his muscles used to carrying or pulling weight and his skin toughened up enough to withstand the pressures and friction of even the best-fitting tack.

continuing a fitness programme

Interval training is still popular, most particularly in the eventing world. Some owners feel that it hypes up hot types too much whereas others say it bores them. All you can do is see if it suits your individual horse.

FOR STARTING OFF a fitness programme see pp.29–33. Once your horse has reached the half-fit stage you can keep his work at two hours a day but decrease the walking and increase the trotting and cantering. By about the twelfth week, he should be able to do two 20-minute trotting spells, plus two 10-minute steady canter spells finishing each spell with a three-quarter-speed canter or 'hand gallop' for half a mile to a mile, without becoming distressed. (Reference to a good book on fitness is advised, see also the feeding information, pp.106–120.) Remember to increase the work before increasing the concentrates, and decrease the concentrates before decreasing the work.

There is no need to give a horse Sunday off if he has worked on Saturday, provided he has not become unduly tired. Three-day event horses do their hardest work on cross-country/steeplechase day but still have to do a respectable show-jumping round on the final day. If your horse works the same way, according to his fitness you could give him Monday off, exercise Tuesday, Wednesday off, exercise Thursday, Friday off (nice and fresh for the weekend), and get away with exercising on only two of your working days of the week, yet still have a reasonably fit horse.

All this assumes that you have adequate turn-out facilities for the non-exercise days. I feel that it is a thoroughly bad practice to leave a horse stabled for even a day without significant exercise (I do not count half an hour leading in hand as significant exercise).

a day off – the facts

Think about it from the horse's point of view. Imagine you dismount at, say, 4pm on Sunday. You plan to give your horse Monday off. If he is stabled, by 4am on Monday he will have had twelve hours without exercise, by 4pm on Monday it will be 24 hours, by 4am on Tuesday morning it will be a mind-boggling 36 hours cooped up in a box without exercise, and if you ride at 7am on Tuesday, the horse will have spent 39 hours (equivalent to a human's full working week) without even enough physical activity to keep his body and soul together. If you do not ride until 6pm on Tuesday evening, your horse will have been subjected to enforced idleness of body and mind for a horrendous 50 hours! That is more than two whole days. So much for a day off – and this could be repeated week after week, month after month.

This, I am sure caring readers will agree, is no way to treat a movement-orientated

exercise and fitness

animal like a horse and the fact that 'everybody does it' doesn't make it right. I think even one day without exercise is a terrible thing for such an animal, who thrives on and needs physical activity for even basic health and contentment. This, if nothing else, should stress how important it is to provide decent turn out facilities and to use them liberally. Time out of his stable is so important that every effort should be made to provide it by riding, driving, lungeing, long-reining, working loose, leading in hand, play-pens or – wait for it – tethering.

tethering That's right. Even if it is only for an hour or two twice a day while you do your horse-chores, a safely tethered horse is surely far more content than one going stir-crazy through being imprisoned in his box. With a little commonsense supervision and assurance from you, he will soon learn all about it, particularly if he is used to being grazed in hand (what livery horse isn't?), to being tied up, or ground-tied so that you can just drop your rope or reins on the ground and he stands still, Western style. Tethering is a logical progression from these.

You must be certain that the horse will not be subject to vandalism, even from the stable dog or loose ponies, and he should not be left out long in adverse weather conditions. Consider using a comfortable neckstrap around his throat rather than a headcollar: many horses seem to prefer them, do not pull on them and they are cheaper. Your tether stake should be the swivel type and be a good yard/metre long – and very firmly driven into the ground. Tethering means you can use any safe piece of grassy ground and, I repeat, is better than no turn out at all.

BE SEEN, BE SAFE

Most working owners in late autumn, winter and early spring have to do most of their exercising in dusk or dark conditions. Floodlit arenas, tracks and indoor schools are wonderful, if you have access to them but many have not.

If you are forced to ride on the road, take a few sensible precautions – they could save lives. Although it is not unlawful in Britain for a horse and rider to go on public roads with no lights, it is extremely stupid – and could lead to claims being made against the rider in the event of an accident; a horse and vehicle must, by law, have lights. I feel that a light is essential in all but the best visibility conditions, along with other high visiblity gear as back up. A stirrup light, showing a strong white light to the front and an equally strong, red one to the rear, with maybe an amber one at the side, depending on the design of light, is ideal for most ridden horses. Keep plenty of batteries handy and take a spare with you. Remember that horses with big bellies may obscure the stirrup light from behind so a better option might be for the rider to use lights on a cyclists' cross-belt.

High-visibility clothing for horse and rider is widely available. Always, day or night, wear the most visible clothing you can, not 'country colours' like brown, green, dark blue or mustard, which blend dangerously with the countryside. Your horse does enough of this for both of you, unless he's light grey. A simple yellow fluorescent tabard is minimal for daytime and the safest thing to have on it is a large red 'L', which keeps traffic wonderfully clear of you.

Quick Reference

This section has been included to help readers find out certain important facts and information quickly.

'Is My Horse Healthy?' gives basic details of a horse's normal 'vital signs' and how to measure them, so that you know what is regarded as normal. It also gives information on various indicators that something is wrong, which should prompt you to phone your vet.

'Should I Call The Vet?' consists of flowcharts that you can follow through to see if a veterinary visit is needed or whether it would be safe to wait to see if things change. However, it is stressed that a phone call to your veterinary practice should produce succinct and helpful advice in any of these situations and that it is far better to do this and be on the safe side than to risk aggravating a health problem through delay.

'Recipes For Success' gives sample day time routines for stabled horses, those at grass and those on the combined system (p.10) for summer and winter. The routines include all essential daily jobs, so nothing will be overlooked if these suggestions are followed.

Lastly, there are a list of useful addresses, giving details of the most useful organizations likely to be needed by most owners, and a decent index. I hope readers will make ready use of the index as many topics are mentioned in several places throughout the book and it will enable you to get all the available information on them quickly.

is my horse healthy?

If you know what is normal, you'll be able to tell what is abnormal. If you have any doubts at all, ring your veterinary practice.

general demeanour	The horse is interested in his surroundings unless sleepy, and is alert but calm; his ears move readily towards anything of interest. He should not appear restless unless something exciting is going on nearby. He should not seem dull and lethargic.
eyes	The horse's eyes are bright and clear with no discharges, swelling, redness, soreness or apparent discomfort, such as frequent rubbing or closing.
condition	General healthy bodyweight means you cannot see your horse's ribs but can feel them easily. In very fit horses, the last few ribs may be seen (depending on type) and the horse will be lean but well muscled up (see also p.122).
skin and coat	The coat is bright, 'lively' and smooth and the skin is pliable, loose and moves easily over ribs under the flat of the hand. A dull, harsh or stiff and raised ('staring') coat indicates ill health, as do spots, sores, bare patches or scabs. Swelling, wounds and raised areas are all abnormal. Outdoor animals may have some scurf and grease in their coat. Frequent rubbing or biting of the skin is a sign of disorder.
action	Should be normal for the individual. This is normally straight, even and level, free and confident. Note existing and old lumps and scars. A hind leg may be rested, but not a foreleg. If the foreleg is held abnormally, forwards, sideways or backwards, suspect a problem. The horse should not be uneasy on his feet, reluctant to bear weight on any foot or be constantly shifting his weight; if his legs or joints are swollen or hot, suspect trouble.
eating and drinking	Study and learn your horse's normal habits so you will know when abnormality arises. Excess saliva or froth from the mouth are abnormal.
droppings	Horse will normally pass droppings about every 2 hours and up to about 12 piles in 24 hours; some breeds, such as Arabs, create more, smaller piles. Normal droppings are apple-sized, oval balls which break on hitting the ground and are khaki to green, never very dark or pale. There should be no slime and they should not be very soft or very hard; strong- or acrid-smelling droppings or blood in the droppings are indicators of problems.
urine	Clear or cloudy, creamy to yellowish. No bad smell or blood. A gelding should drop his penis to stale (pass urine).
respiration	Barely noticeable in a healthy, resting horse. It should be silent and smooth. If rapid at rest or unusually noisy, suspect a problem.
nose	Very slight, watery discharge, particularly after exercise, is normal. Excessive or thick discharge or blood is abnormal. Yellow, green or thick discharge indicates an infection. Food coming down one or both nostrils can indicate a serious problem, such as choke.

vital signs	**Temperature, pulse and respiration rates:** Get to know your horse's temperature, pulse (heart) and respiration rates at rest, immediately after work and during recovery from work. Take them at the same time each day under the same conditions for a week (this takes about five minutes) so that you know his average readings. Below are the average at-rest rates for a horse. Healthy ponies, youngsters and unfit animals will have higher rates than healthy horses, old or fit animals.
temperature	About 38°C (100.4°F) **To take a temperature:** Obtain a thermometer from your vet (digital or ordinary veterinary type). With the latter, shake the mercury well down with a snapping movement of your wrist. Moisten the end of the thermometer (with spit or petroleum jelly). Stand behind and to the left of the horse, pull the top of the dock towards you with your left hand and insert the thermometer into the anus with a gentle twisting, side-to-side movement. Press it gently against the wall of the rectum and leave in place for the time stated. Gently remove it, wipe clean quickly on the tail and read the temperature.
pulse	About 32 to 42 beats per minute (bpm) **To take the pulse:** The pulse can be felt where an artery crosses a bone (under the jawbone, inside the elbow a little way down, above the eye and under or at the side of the dock about a third of the way down). Find a pulse by feeling with your fingers and then leaving them in place for a few seconds. Using a watch with a second hand, count the beats for 30 seconds, then double the result.
respiration	About 8 to 14 breaths per minute (in and out counts as one breath) **To measure the respiration:** Stand behind and slightly to one side of the horse and watch his opposite flank rise and fall (can be difficult to spot), or hold up a mirror to a nostril and, once the horse is used to this, count how often it steams up in a minute.

WARNING SIGNS

Every time you visit your horse check for signs of restlessness; in a stable these include disturbed bedding and scrape marks on the wall. Check the state of his food and water, and consider his general demeanour.

- **After rolling** *your horse should get up and shake himself, if he doesn't this may indicate he has colic. More rolling than usual can also mean abdominal pain.*

- **Patchy sweating** *can be caused by pain.*

- **Cold sweat** *is a sign of fatigue or shock.*

- **Dehydration** *is checked by pressing your thumb firmly on the gum to create a pale patch – the colour (blood) should return within 2 seconds or less. If it takes longer than this, the horse is probably dehydrated, in shock or losing blood/blood pressure. Also, pinch up and twist a fold of skin on the side of the neck or point of shoulder: in a healthy horse, it falls flat immediately on letting go. (See also p.109.)*

In any of these situations call your vet for advice or to arrange a visit.

should I call the vet?

These flowcharts will help you decide whether to request a visit from your vet or whether it should be safe to wait a while. **However, it is far better to call your vet and ask for advice than to risk aggravating a problem through delay.**

bleeding

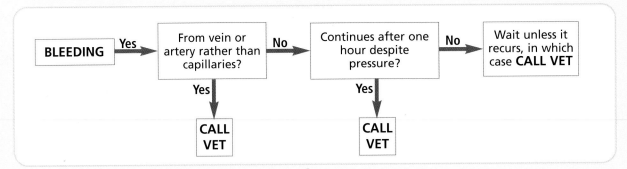

BLEEDING → **Yes** → From vein or artery rather than capillaries? → **No** → Continues after one hour despite pressure? → **No** → Wait unless it recurs, in which case **CALL VET**

From vein or artery rather than capillaries? → **Yes** → **CALL VET**

Continues after one hour despite pressure? → **Yes** → **CALL VET**

breathing

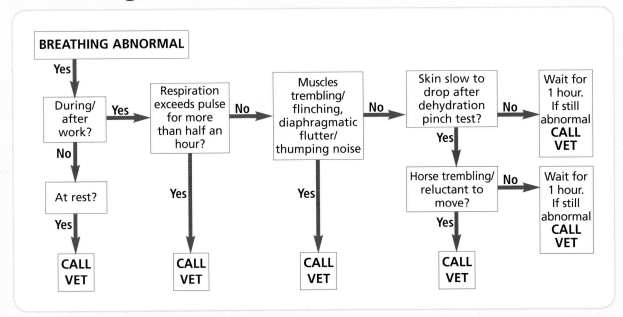

BREATHING ABNORMAL → **Yes** → During/after work? → **Yes** → Respiration exceeds pulse for more than half an hour? → **No** → Muscles trembling/flinching, diaphragmatic flutter/thumping noise → **No** → Skin slow to drop after dehydration pinch test? → **No** → Wait for 1 hour. If still abnormal **CALL VET**

During/after work? → **No** → At rest? → **Yes** → **CALL VET**

Respiration exceeds pulse for more than half an hour? → **Yes** → **CALL VET**

Muscles trembling/flinching, diaphragmatic flutter/thumping noise → **Yes** → **CALL VET**

Skin slow to drop after dehydration pinch test? → **Yes** → Horse trembling/reluctant to move? → **No** → Wait for 1 hour. If still abnormal **CALL VET**

Horse trembling/reluctant to move? → **Yes** → **CALL VET**

coughing

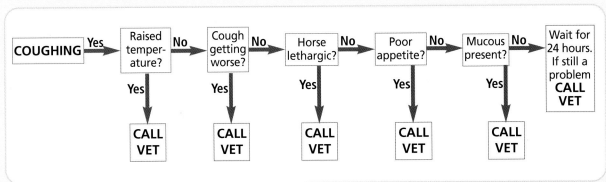

COUGHING → **Yes** → Raised temperature? → **No** → Cough getting worse? → **No** → Horse lethargic? → **No** → Poor appetite? → **No** → Mucous present? → **No** → Wait for 24 hours. If still a problem **CALL VET**

Raised temperature? → **Yes** → **CALL VET**

Cough getting worse? → **Yes** → **CALL VET**

Horse lethargic? → **Yes** → **CALL VET**

Poor appetite? → **Yes** → **CALL VET**

Mucous present? → **Yes** → **CALL VET**

choking/salivation

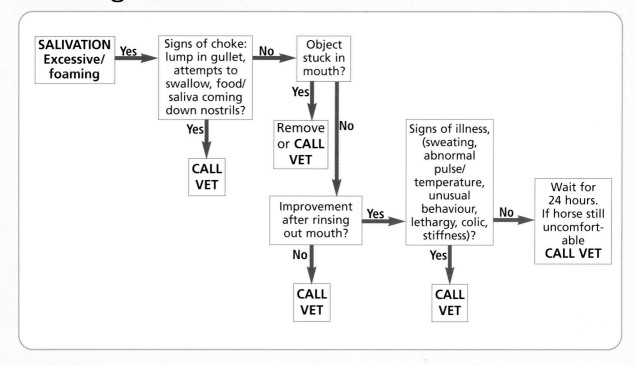

digestion

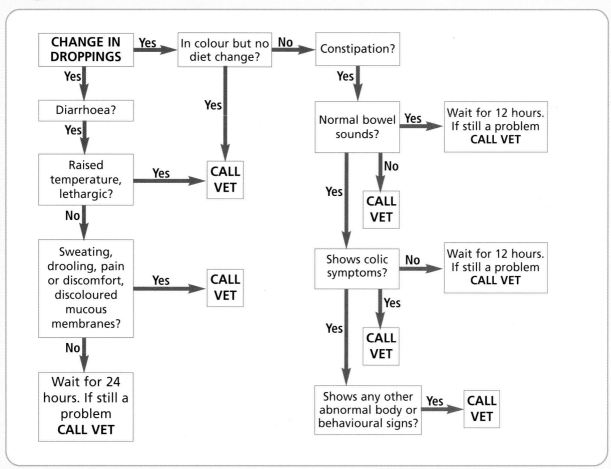

should I get the vet?

gait/action

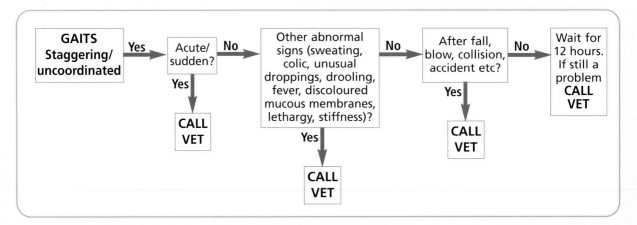

GAITS Staggering/ uncoordinated → **Yes** → Acute/ sudden? → **Yes** → **CALL VET**

Acute/sudden? → **No** → Other abnormal signs (sweating, colic, unusual droppings, drooling, fever, discoloured mucous membranes, lethargy, stiffness)? → **Yes** → **CALL VET**

Other abnormal signs? → **No** → After fall, blow, collision, accident etc? → **Yes** → **CALL VET**

After fall, blow, collision, accident etc? → **No** → Wait for 12 hours. If still a problem **CALL VET**

lameness

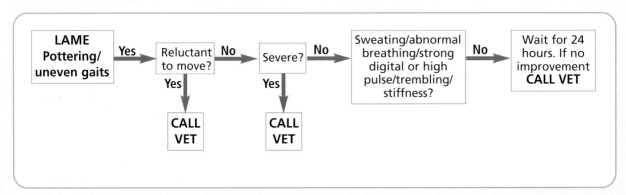

LAME Pottering/ uneven gaits → **Yes** → Reluctant to move? → **Yes** → **CALL VET**

Reluctant to move? → **No** → Severe? → **Yes** → **CALL VET**

Severe? → **No** → Sweating/abnormal breathing/strong digital or high pulse/trembling/ stiffness? → **No** → Wait for 24 hours. If no improvement **CALL VET**

swelling

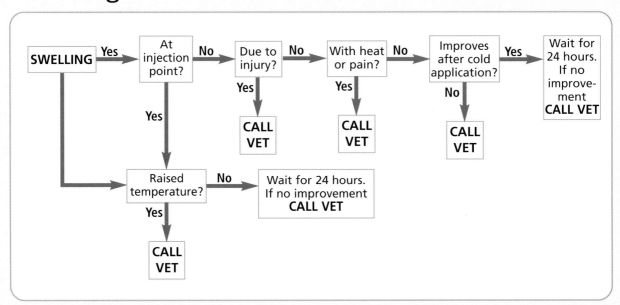

SWELLING → **Yes** → At injection point? → **Yes** → Raised temperature?

SWELLING → (down) → Raised temperature? → **Yes** → **CALL VET**

Raised temperature? → **No** → Wait for 24 hours. If no improvement **CALL VET**

At injection point? → **No** → Due to injury? → **Yes** → **CALL VET**

Due to injury? → **No** → With heat or pain? → **Yes** → **CALL VET**

With heat or pain? → **No** → Improves after cold application? → **No** → **CALL VET**

Improves after cold application? → **Yes** → Wait for 24 hours. If no improvement **CALL VET**

temperature

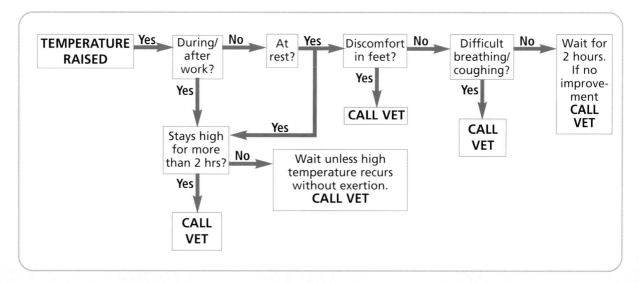

urine

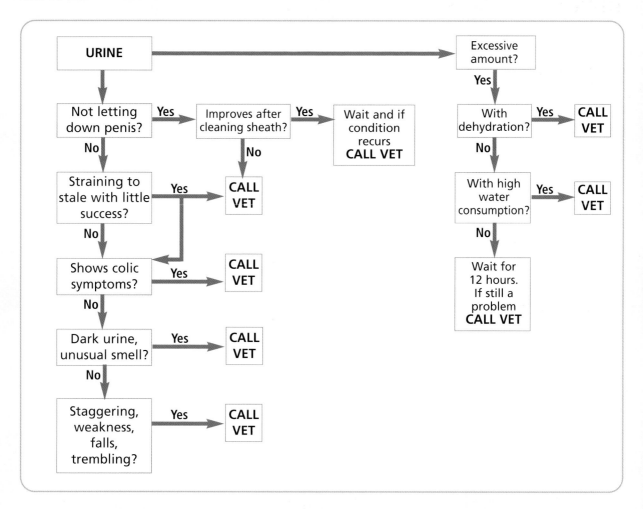

recipes for success

It is useful to have an established routine for each time you visit your horse, this enables you to be more efficient and also makes sure that you don't forget something vital. These routines are suggestions of successful ways of doing everything that needs to be done daily. Tack can be cleaned at home, rather than wasting 'stables' time. Other jobs can be done at weekends or on non-exercise days. **All essential daily jobs are listed here:** by following these routines and fitting them in with your own life, you can be sure you are doing everything necessary to care for your horse quite adequately. However, use the lists of A and B jobs (pp.68–69) to help you prioritize, too. And don't forget to put your horse's comfort first.

stabled horse	**The most time-consuming routine. Ignore references to winter clothing in summer. Otherwise, this routine is suitable all year round.**	
early morning	• Check for signs of normality or otherwise. Check droppings for consistency, odour, colour and number. Check box for signs of restlessness (churned-up bedding, scrape marks on walls), which could indicate that the horse has been cast during the night or had colic. Check the hay is eaten, feed finished and water drunk. Takes one minute only. • Skip out droppings or muck out, leaving floor bare. • Quarter and pick out feet. • Tack up or harness and put to, including light and high-visibility gear, if appropriate.	• Exercise. If it's raining and cold, trot home to keep him warm. • On return, put away tack, hang clothing to dry. Put on permeable rugs in winter if the horse is wet. • Give a very full haynet/tub or two. • Bed down or add new material to existing bed. • Give two buckets of water/check automatic waterer. • Feed. • Leave midday feed/hay for helper to give, if appropriate. • Leave for work.
midday (if help available)	• Rug up horse normally or adjust rugs. • Skip out.	• Feed/hay/water.
evening	• Check as early morning. • Quarter, pick out feet. • Tack up or harness and put to, including light and high-visibility gear, if appropriate. • Exercise/work in hand or loose, lead out to graze. • On return, put away equipment.	• Put on permeable rug if the horse is wet in winter. • Check feet. • Give water/hay. • Skip out/replenish bedding. • Groom dry parts. • Feed.
late evening	• Check as usual. • Rug up normally/adjust rugs. • Leave double hay ration and two buckets of water/check automatic waterer. • Skip out/fluff up bedding.	• Groom, if not done before. • Feed, if required. • Leave dry feeds mixed for morning/full haynets. • Take exercise clothing home to dry,
horse at grass	**The routine for a grass-kept horse is not quite so tying and time-sensitive as for a stabled horse but still needs doing!**	
winter notes	If the horse is a tough type, living out without rug or shelter, extra vigilance is needed. He cannot be clipped and will seldom be dry enough to put on tack, so weekday exercise will be omitted. Check especially for demeanour, chill, bodyweight and ailments. Check feet and legs daily.	
daily routine	If the horse is expected to do moderate work at weekends, he will need exercise on two or three days weekly to maintain fitness. Suggested routine for exercise day:	

winter early morning	• Tie up in shelter or spare stable and remove turnout rug. Feel right through unclipped areas of his coat to check condition. Pick out feet and tidy up as best you can. • Specially look for signs of chill and exposure ailments, such as mud fever, rain scald and runny eyes or a chapped face.	• Tack up or harness and put to, maybe with lights and reflective gear. A light, waterproof sheet will be needed if it's raining as a turnout rug cannot be replaced on a wet coat unless it is permeable. • On return, feed, top up forage, check water, skip out shelter. Replace rug. • Put away gear, hang exercise sheet to dry.
winter evening	• Check horse. Quarter and check feet, looking specially for exposure ailments. • If possible, bring him in and feed while you rinse off mud, dry thoroughly and apply preventative	cream, if he is susceptible to skin problems. • Replace dry rug and return to field. • Top up hay, check water, skip out shelter, replenish bedding.
summer early morning	• Check horse, quarter, pick out feet. Tack up or harness and put to. • Exercise.	• On return, feed if appropriate, skip out shelter, check water, put hay in the shelter if grass sparse. • Put away equipment.
summer evening	• Check horse, quarter and pick out feet. • If exercising, tack up or harness, put to and exercise.	• On return, feed if appropriate, skip out shelter, check water, hay up shelter if necessary. • Put away equipment.
combined system	**Probably the best system for horse and owner. The routine here is for a horse that is trace or chaser clipped in winter.**	
winter early morning	• Check as for stabled horse. Quarter, pick out feet. • Tack up or harness and put to, using high-visibility gear if appropriate. • Exercise, using waterproof sheet if it's raining. • On return, put away tack and feed horse.	• Put exercise clothing to dry. Put on turnout rug. • Fill up shelter hay supply, check water and leave midday feed for helper to give, if possible. • Turn out horse. • Muck out stable, leaving floor bare, or skip out.
winter evening	• Bed down/replenish bedding, put in double hay supply and two buckets of water, or check automatic waterer. • Bring horse in, remove turnout rug and check carefully for injuries/ailments.	• Quarter/groom and rug up for night. • If necessary, wash, dry and cream legs as for grass-kept horse. Otherwise, bandage legs. • Put turnout rug somewhere to dry.
winter late evening (if possible)	• Check horse, adjust rugs. • Top up hay/water. • Skip out and fluff up bedding.	• Feed, if required, and leave dry feed ready for morning.
summer early morning	• Bed down/replenish bedding. • Bring horse in and check. • Quarter/groom, pick out feet and check shoes. • If exercising, tack up or harness and put to.	• Exercise. On return, put away equipment, provide feed, double hay and water. • Leave horse in for the day, away from sun and flies.
summer midday	• Check horse • Skip out	• Feed/hay/water
summer evening	• Check horse, feed if appropriate and turn out for the night. • Muck out, leave floor bare overnight, or skip out.	• Skip out shelter, replenish bedding. • Check water, hay up shelter if paddock bare.

useful addresses & further reading

The British Horse Society
Stoneleigh Deer Park
Kenilworth
Warwickshire CV8 2XZ

Association of British Riding Schools
Queens Chambers
38-40 Queen Street
Penzance
Cornwall TR18 RBH

Association of Chartered Physiotherapists in Animal Therapy
Morland House
Salters Lane
Winchester
Hampshire SO22 5JP

Association of Riding Establishments of Northern Ireland
126 Monlough Road
Saintfield
County Down
BT24 7EU

British Association of Holistic Nutrition and Medicine
Borough Court
Hartley Wintney
Basingstoke
Hampshire RG27 8JA

British Association of Homoeopathic Veterinary Surgeons
Chinham House
Stanford-in-the-Vale
Faringdon
Oxfordshire SN7 8NQ

British Equestrian Trade Association
Stockeld Park
Wetherby
West Yorkshire LS22 4AW

British Equine Veterinary Association
5 Finlay Street
London SW6 6HE

Equilibrium Products
Unit 7
Upper Wingbury Farm
Leighton Road
Wingrave
Buckinghamshire HP22 4LW

Equine Behaviour Forum
Grove Cottage
Brinkley
Newmarket
Suffolk CB8 0SF

Equine Lawyers Association
PO Box 23
Brigg
North Lincolnshire DN20 8TN

The Farriers Registration Council
Sefton House, Adam Court
Newark Road
Peterborough
Cambridgeshire PE1 5PP

Institute of Grassland and Environmental Research
Plas Goggerdan
Aberystwyth
Ceredigion SY23 3EB

The Insurance Ombudsman
City Gate One
135 Park Street
London SE1 9EA

National Institute of Medical Herbalists
56 Longbrook Street
Exeter
Devon EX4 6AH

Open Spaces Society
25a Bell Street
Henley-on-Thames
Oxfordshire RG9 2BA

The Organisation of Horsebox and Trailer Owners
Whitehill Farm
Hamstead Marshall
Newbury
Berkshire RG20 0HP

Riders of Britain
South View Equestrian Centre
Winsford Road
Wettenhall
Cheshire CW7 4DL

Riding for The Disabled Association
Lavinia Norfolk House
Avenue R
National Agricultural Centre
Stoneleigh Park
Kenilworth
Warwickshire CV8 2LY

Royal College of Veterinary Surgeons
Belgravia House
62–4 Horseferry Road
London SW1P 2AF

Saddler's Company
40 Gutter Lane
London EC2V 6BR

Society of Master Saddlers (UK) Ltd.
Kettles Farm
Mickfield
Stowmarket
Suffolk IP14 6BY

Further Reading

Essential Care of the Ridden Horse
Peter Gray
The Organic Horse
Peter Gray
Complementary Therapies for Horse and Rider
Susan McBane & Caroline Davis
Feeding Horses & Ponies
Susan McBane
How Your Horse Works
Susan McBane
The Essential Book of Horse Tack & Equipment
Susan McBane
Keeping a Horse Outdoors
Susan McBane

Acknowledgements

All photographs by Horsepix except the following:

Abigail Hogg p10
Peter Sweet p11
Equilibrium p24(btm)
David & Charles/Andrew Perkins pp 45, 109(rt), 123(lft), 127
David & Charles/Kit Houghton p55
Susan McBane pp 75(rt), 95, 122
Shona Wallis p91(lower set of photographs)
Kit Houghton p113
Colin Vogel p131

Artworks on pp96–7 by Maggie Raynor

index

Doing a Literature Search